# The
# Buckinghamshire
# Village Book

*Other volumes in this series include*

THE NEW BERKSHIRE VILLAGE BOOK
BFWI

THE DORSET VILLAGE BOOK
Harry Ashley

THE EAST SUSSEX VILLAGE BOOK
Rupert Taylor

THE GLOUCESTERSHIRE VILLAGE BOOK
GFWI

THE HAMPSHIRE VILLAGE BOOK
Anthony Brode

THE KENT VILLAGE BOOK
Alan Bignell

THE OXFORDSHIRE VILLAGE BOOK
Nigel Hammond

THE SUFFOLK VILLAGE BOOK
Harold Mills West

THE SURREY VILLAGE BOOK
Graham Collyer

THE WEST SUSSEX VILLAGE BOOK
Tony Wales

# The Buckinghamshire Village Book

With Illustrations by Claudia Gaukroger

Compiled by the Buckinghamshire
Federation of Women's Institutes
from notes sent by
Institutes in the County

Published jointly by
Countryside Books, Newbury
and the BFWI, High Wycombe

First Published 1987

© Buckinghamshire Federation of Women's Institutes 1987

Countryside Books
3 Catherine Road
Newbury, Berkshire

ISBN 0 905392 80 9

Cover photograph of Ellesborough
by Alicia Sargeant

Produced through MRM (Print Consultants) Ltd., Reading
Typeset by Acorn Bookwork, Salisbury
Printed in England by J. W. Arrowsmith, Bristol

# Foreword

Welcome to Buckinghamshire.

The County is one of contrasts. In the south it is crossed by the beechwood covered chalk ridge of the Chiltern Hills. Here in the spring bluebells and cherry blossom abound. To the north of these hills the Vale of Aylesbury is one of England's richest agricultural regions. It is a County which, despite the influx of London commuters and the growth of the new city of Milton Keynes, still retains its villages, farmlands and towns of character and charm.

Buckinghamshire is steeped in history and has associations with the famous – John Milton, Benjamin Disraeli and the Rothschilds to name but a few.

To produce this book many members of the Buckinghamshire Federation of Women's Institutes have undertaken a great deal of research and in order to cover the whole of the County and where no W.I. exists, non members have also willingly contributed. It has been a pleasurable task; we are most grateful to them all and must apologise to those whose efforts have not been included through lack of space.

It is hoped that readers of this book will stop in our villages, explore them and leave a little richer for the experience.

Beryl Brown
*County Federation Chairman*

# County of Buckinghamshire

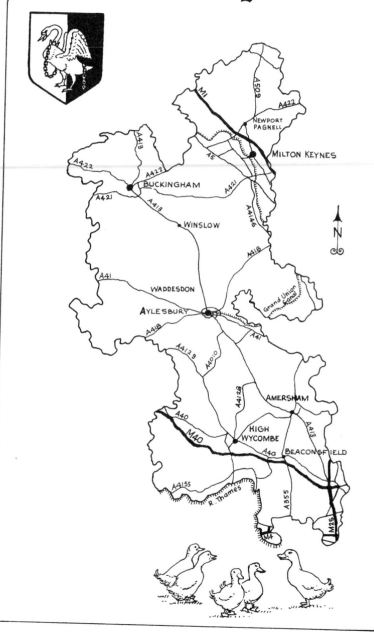

# Acknowledgements

The Buckinghamshire Federation of Women's Institutes wish to thank all Institutes whose members worked to provide the information about their villages, and the following who provided additional material:

Hedgerley Historical Association (Hedgerley)
Arthur Reeve (Marsworth)
Jim Lancaster (North Crawley)
Miles Green & John Broadbent (Penn & Tylers Green)
Alice Dean (Speen)
Norman Carr (Waddesdon)
Donald Varney (Part of West Wycombe)
Alicia Sargeant (Cover photograph of Ellesborough)
Claudia Gaukroger (for all the illustrations)

Finally, a special thank you to Nan Johnson, the co-ordinator of the project.

The Grand Union Canal near Marsworth

# Akeley

Akeley derives its name from 'Ake', the Anglo-Saxon word for Oak, and 'Ley', a field. In the Domesday Book it is spelled Achelei. Akeley had a church in 1164 and its living came into the possession of Longueville Abbey.

Of the interesting people who were buried at Akeley one was a Miss Ann Clark, who died at the age of 104 years. She saw no less than seven kings and queens on the throne of England, being born in the reign of Charles II and dying in the reign of George III. Akeley used to be noted for its lace industry. It had a large school for teaching the children the art of pillow lace making in cottages opposite the Grey Hound public house which was also the village bakery. It is now closed and has been converted into a private house.

Akeley also possessed a flourishing brickyard and pottery in the early part of the 19th century. This was owned by a Mr and Mrs Barton who specialized in making flower pots, drain pipes for the building trade, and ornamental pedestals, bread bins and bricks etc. The clay was dug from a field at the back of the Pits, which used to have water at the bottom. The kiln stood for a number of years after the brick yard closed. The property was owned by a Mr Watts who had a large house and orchard in the village where some of the ornamental bricks were used in the garden walls. There was also a butcher with its own slaughter house, two shoe repairers, one post office and shop and another shop selling a large selection of goods and food.

During the First World War hundreds of horses taken from the farms and land were re-shod before being shipped off to the battle front in France. Milk was delivered straight from the farm to houses in milk buckets and ladled into customers' jugs etc. Two coal and wood dealers used to make up faggots of wood. A local builder also made coffins.

Akeley Church was built in 1854 and the Methodist Chapel was built in 1829. The church was pulled down in 1979 owing to the rotting stone and the chapel closed down in 1986.

In Akeley Wood there is a very large school which was built on a large estate which was built by Mr C. Pilgrim Esq. and has changed ownership over the years.

The main event of the village social life was the Horticultural Show which was considered the best in North Buckinghamshire. This closed down in 1918 but was restarted in 1976 and is once again a popular social village event.

# Ashendon 🌿

Ashendon, which includes the tiny hamlets of Upper and Lower Pollicott, is a small, friendly village which has changed relatively little in living memory. Built high on a ridge, it has magnificent views across the Vale of Aylesbury, particularly from the grounds of the 12th century church. The stone and brick cottages, some even thatched, convey the impression of an age old settlement, and indeed the 'place of ash trees on the hill' appears to have been of some importance in Saxon times.

Ashendon can boast of no 'big house' or well known personality, but it is a complete village, with its church, shop and public house, and the seven original farms still being worked, one of which has been farmed by the same family for at least 350 years. In the early part of the century a roadman was asked where a gentleman of the name of George lived; he replied, 'There b'aint no gentlemen in Ashendon, they be all farmers!' Agriculture remains the only industry in the village, and there are still several of the old village families left.

Although there is very little population movement, there is a good mix of old and new inhabitants, the newer ones always welcomed into the many and varied village activities. The traditional Ashendon Feast is alas now a distant memory of the past, recalled only by inhabitants in their late seventies and eighties. This was a great day to look forward to, always held on the first Tuesday in May, and folk used to say the weather would never warm up until after the Feast. The children were up bright and early, many going to the top of Lynch Hill to catch a first glimpse of the Fair people. A roundabout was soon erected in the Hanger, and swinging boats in the Square. Coconut shies ran parallel with the garden hedge of Cherry Cottage, and an old lady frying an inexhaustible supply of sausages was always part of the scene. Salt beef and ham were eaten in the evening at Ashendon Farm.

In 1962 a new village tradition began, orginally to celebrate the belated hanging of a gate into the allotments. The gate had lain in the hedge for several years, and at last two villagers fixed it in place. It was decided that a dinner should be arranged to mark the occasion, and each year since then the men of the village have met for the Ashendon Gatehangers dinner. Over the years the Gatehangers have helped the village in many ways, including gifts to the OAP's at Christmas, visits and gifts to people in hospital, and donations to help start the football club and to the Village Hall.

# Ashley Green

The village of Ashley Green is situated on the B416 road running from Berkhamsted to Chesham. It is one of the typical Chiltern villages, consisting of a long 'green', with a church, post office/ shop, village hall and public house. Unfortunately, it is dissected by the main road.

The soil is clay, in chalk flints, and there are many underground rivers and streams in the area. There are also underground sandstone caves in the village. These are filled with water most of the year round it is supposed, and no one seems to know where the entrance to the caves is, although it is strongly suspected that the entrance is in a small area near the green, now owned by the Water Board. It is also thought that from the caves leads a passageway to Berkhamsted Castle.

The village green has a couple of interesting features. There is a pond at the east side of the green. There is a pudding stone on the green itself near a horse chestnut tree, marking the depth of a well. The pudding stone was moved to the green when the church was built. Originally it had stood on the site where the church now is for centuries and three lay lines crossed the spot where the stone stood.

Much wildlife can be found surrounding the village. Badger setts are frequent, and the muntjac deer are increasing, often entering larger gardens.

# Aston Clinton 🌿

Aston Clinton is a large village nestling in the lee of the Chiltern Hills some 4 miles east of Aylesbury. It is traversed by the busy A41 trunk road with its tremendous volume of traffic.

The inhabitants mostly commute to the larger towns as there is little industry nearby. The saw mill owned by Mr Weston has long since disappeared, so has the wood-turning business run by Mr Marriott, who turned chair legs and sent them by the load to High Wycombe.

Just over seventy years ago Mr Howe ran a horse bus to Aylesbury and operated from the house now owned by the Raglan Kennels. In 1919 he acquired a motor bus which ran twice daily to the market town. However, the horse and cart was still the main mode of travel and the blacksmith had premises in the Main Street on the site of what is now Madge Garage, and the wheelwright resided further down the road. The present Partridge Arms was the home of the saddler.

Motor vehicles became more sophisticated and a maker by the name of Martin used to race his cars up Aston Hill; thus the name of Aston Martin was derived. This hill now forms part of the land owned and managed by the Forestry Commission.

Lords of the Manor, or Squires, include the medieval Minshull family, Lord Luke of Delhi, and Sir Anthony de Rothschild. It is the latter, one of the four sons of Nathan Maye de Rothschild, who is best remembered.

He came to live in Aston Clinton in 1853 and amongst his achievements was the establishment of the Chiltern Hills Spring Water Company. The Buckland, Drayton Beauchamp and Aston Clinton W.I. meet in the Anthony Hall, now a listed building, which was given to the village by Lady de Rothschild in memory of her husband.

It contains a painting of his two daughters Connie and Annie, who as children discovered that whereas boys were educated in the church school, girls were only allowed to attend a straw plaiting school situated in the main street. Although aged only eleven and nine respectively, the de Rothschild children took it upon themselves to teach the girls. Sir Anthony came to the rescue and built a girls school and subsequently, at her request, gave Connie an infants school for her sixteenth birthday present. The boys school was rebuilt in 1887 and is surmounted by the Jubilee Clock, which was erected to commemorate the Diamond Jubilee of Queen Victoria.

By a quirk of nature, the village has suffered three whirlwinds. One in 1950 when extensive damage was done, including the lifting of the school roof, causing the school to be closed, one in the late 1970s and one in 1984. The latter ripped off roofs, moved fences and garden sheds, splintered greenhouses and bent many a television aerial.

Although the adjoining parishes of Buckland and Drayton Beauchamp retain their independence, they have associations with Aston Clinton and share some of its amenities.

# Ballinger & South Heath

Standing on the hills above Great Missenden are the pleasantly rural villages of Ballinger and South Heath. The small village church of St Marys at Ballinger is very quaint and old and has been carefully looked after through the many years by devoted villagers.

The Ballinger War Memorial Hall gives quite a lot of entertainment, as this is the meeting place of many societies. This hall has given much pleasure to many of us who have lived in the community all our lives. As children we were very lucky as Ballinger Grange was a large Boarding School and the teachers would give up their Saturday afternoons to teach us to dance and take part in plays which were held in the Memorial Hall, as were the most wonderful Christmas parties.

Ballinger and South Heath also had a very good orchestra with some twenty odd players, it was quite a night out when they put their concerts on.

The W.I. started many years ago as an afternoon group and much canning and jam making was done during the Second World War from fruit that was grown locally.

We have two village shops with post office services in Ballinger and South Heath which is really quite rare in these days. As these have survived for sixty or more years, this adds so much to the community.

We have had many good craftsmen in the locality. Some of the most fascinating were those that laid hedges and thatched hay-stacks. Fortunately the craft of hedge-laying seems to be returning, and together with the new wild life conservation these hedges are giving our wild birds more cover.

Ballinger also had a very good blacksmith, and in South Heath we had one of the early lace-makers. This craft again is reviving with various groups locally.

We had wonderful cherry orchards, especially in Ballinger, and the crops were excellent. As children we used to go and get baskets full for preserving and making the famous Black Cherry Pies. These were the boast of the local housewives. Now sadly just a few skeleton trees remain.

A ghostly story of South Heath is told that on a certain night a coach and four horses drives from behind Bury Farm in Potter Row down the driveway across the road and disappears into the mists of the field beyond.

# Beachampton

Beachampton is in low-lying ground west of Milton Keynes in the north of Buckinghamshire. The name has changed little since Beachampton was mentioned in the Domesday Book. In 1086 there were 30 heads of households recorded making a population of 100–120. By 1871 there were 272 inhabitants and lace-making was mentioned as a chief occupation of the females. Today the population is about 150 persons. Most people are employed in Milton Keynes though there are some jobs on local farms.

After the Norman Conquest the Manor of Beachampton was given to Walter Giffard, Commander of the Norman Army at the Battle of Hastings. A Manor House was in existence by 1333 and at that time there were two water mills – a name recalled by the present Mill Farm on the Stony Stratford Road.

Subsequently the Manor passed to the Cecils, the Marquess of Salisbury selling the estate in 1807. Later it was inherited by the Walker family and remained in their ownership until it was broken up at an auction in 1922.

The best starting point for a tour of the village is the church. It is The Church of the Assumption of St Mary the Virgin and dates from the 14th century. The whole building was extensively restored by the Victorian architect G. E. Street.

On leaving the church by the main gate, look into the field opposite. The wall and gateway are those of Hall Farm, the former Manor House. In this field Queen Anne is said to have inspected some of her troops.

The present 17th century stone built farmhouse was an addition to the Tudor Manor House. That, according to tradition, was the home of Catherine Parr, sixth wife of King Henry VIII. The earlier building was largely dismantled in the 18th century and some material used for farm outbuildings.

On the opposite side of the road is Beachampton Place, formerly the Victorian Rectory. Now continue down the lane and, before turning right into Main Street for the village, look ahead to Manor Farm. The stone built farmhouse dates from the 17th century.

As you walk down Main Street, you will pass the one remaining thatched cottage in Beachampton, although old photographs show that other houses, including the inn, were originally thatched.

The Old School on the opposite side of the road was built in 1869. It closed in the 1920s and is now a private house and the Village Hall. On the right are four Victorian cottages, originally built for workers on Beachampton Estate. The one with a post box by its gate was the village post office and shop.

# Bellingdon

Bellingdon is a small village about a mile out of Chesham on a ridge of the Chiltern Hills, 600 feet above sea level.

Before the Second World War this was a close-knit community with most of the villagers employed in farming and brick-making. The squire was Mr William Lowndes who lived at The Bury in Chesham.

The annual fete was held in the squire's grounds and it was greatly looked forward to as there were so few amusements in those days.

The children walked to the next village at Asheridge to attend school. There were no buses and they walked through the fields and looked for the first honeysuckle leaves in the spring and they knew where the birds' nests were.

Their parents grew all the vegetables in their gardens and they had cherry, apple and plum trees as well. They were able to find wild raspberries and crabapples in the woods.

The church is still the centre of the village activities. It is a small wooden building about 100 years old.

There used to be two public houses, The Bull and The Golden Perch. The latter one was demolished years ago.

About 50 houses have been built since the war, reducing the farmland. Small farms have been taken over by larger farms. Far fewer men are needed on the farms and they now work in the factories in Chesham or commute 'up the line' to London by car or train.

The Village Hall was built 38 years ago on ground given by Miss Marian Thompson, the first W.I. President. The Hall is well used by the various village societies.

Bellingdon villagers are keen gardeners and the annual horticultural show has an extremely high standard. The Hall is bursting at the seams when this is held as besides the wonderful displays of vegetables and flowers there are competitions for preserves and cakes, sewing and knitting and entries for the children's miniature gardens and animals made from vegetables.

# Bledlow 🐖

Bledlow is a conservation village and thus retains much of its original pattern. It now includes the hamlets of Skittle Green, Forty Green, Holly Green and Pitch Green all of which lie north of the busy B4009, the Lower Icknield Way.

Though the origins of the village can be traced to the 10th century, there is clear evidence of earlier occupation. Close to the Upper Icknield Way is a Bronze Age barrow known locally as 'The Cop' which was excavated in 1938. One mile south of the village is Bledlow Cross, carved out of the Chiltern Ridge by the Anglo-Saxons and, with its neighbour Whiteleaf Cross, are the only turf-cut crosses in the country.

After the Norman Conquest, William I granted the Manor of Bledlow to his half-brother Robert, who held it in 1086. In the reign of Henry VI it was granted to Eton College but in 1650 James Blanck became owner and he built the original Manor House. Records show that the present Manor was sold in 1801 to Lord Carrington whose successor holds it at the present day.

The Wesleyan Methodist Chapel in Chapel Lane was built in

1869. In 1913 a schoolroom was added on reclaimed marshland where older residents of Bledlow can recall skating on frozen water. The Chapel provides the village with its Sunday School attended by many young children in the schoolroom.

The main Village School was built in 1868 and celebrated its centenary before closure in 1973 and subsequent demolition in 1984. Miss E. M. Folley had almost 52 years association with the school as both pupil and teacher. Present primary children must travel some 2 miles to Longwick. Five new flint and brick houses now stand on the site of the old school.

Bledlow has many listed buildings. The 16th century timber framed houses built near the church show the decorative Elizabethan brick herringboning but 'The Cottage' in West Lane is reputed to be the oldest house in the village of ancient cruck construction. It was once 2 cottages, the older of which is some 600 years old.

In 1977 a small development of retirement homes built on the site of the old village shop won for the Architects much publicity and an award from the R.I.B.A.

Now, although the old names of Heybourn, Gomme and Tappin are still here, most residents are commuters either to London, High Wycombe or Aylesbury. Like many villages it has become a haven of rural living rather than a bustling village where people once were born, lived, worked and died; where the village was a self-sufficient entity within its own community.

# Bledlow Ridge

Bledlow Ridge is a long stretch of roadway that winds up a steep ascent from West Wycombe over the Chiltern Hills towards Oxfordshire. It is part of the ancient parish of Bledlow and gets a mention in the Domesday Book. The name means 'Bloody Hill' and commemorates a fierce battle between the Danes and the Saxons. It goes further back into history than that. Impressions exist of hut circles and the occasional fragments of pottery and implements, which together with the nearness of the Icknield Way, indicate a Romano-British settlement of around 300 BC. From time to time, iron cannon balls, silver shoe buckles and coin of the early Stuart kings are unearthed, evidence of a battle between the Royalists and the Roundheads in the Civil War and the famous victory for the Royalists at Chinnor in 1643.

Bledlow Ridge was mostly common land in those days. On the common stood an Elizabethan farmhouse where Cromwell stabled his horse in one of the adjoining barns. As recently as the last couple of decades, a sword of the period was discovered concealed in the wide chimney of an open fireplace. Pankridge now faces onto a busy road, no longer a farm but an integral part of the village and centre of many social gatherings.

In 1917, Loxborough House at the top of Loxborough Hill, once regarded as the Manor House, was acquired by a Mr Henry O'Reilly Stevens, the maker of the famous Stevens Ink. The grounds were a popular venue for garden parties and similar festivities that raised money for village needs. By this means a Parish Institute was built.

There are houses on the Ridge that date from over 300 years ago. Among these was The Old Mansion noted for a large loft where fleeces were stored for collection by woolpack men who plied their trade between Wantage and London. Three of these nomadic people named Brooks squatted on nearby land called The Scrubbs. Several families all bearing the same name was the result, making it necessary to distinguish them by adding the name of their dwelling or occupation. Some had Bible names – Able, Isaac and even Moses. The name 'The City' mystifies newcomers. There are two explanations: refugees fleeing from the City of London sought protection there from the Great Plague of 1666 or it was a hideout for a City Guild with good reason to escape from the Bow Street Runners.

Changes took place at The Old Mansion in 1918 when Sir William and Lady Lister bought it as a country residence. A nephew of Lord Lister of antiseptics fame, Sir William was consulting oculist to King George V and surgeon oculist to His Majesty's Household. During the Second World War, Sir William developed a portable electro-magnetic device for removing foreign bodies from the eye.

Bledlow Ridge W.I. has earned a place in local history for its phenomenal jam making record during the Second World War. They produced 25 cwt. from a glut of cottage garden grown greengages the like of which had never been known before or since. Their efforts received high praise from the County. What price the 'Jam and Jerusalem' image then?

# Booker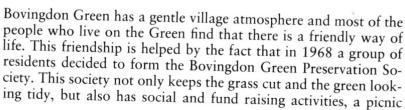

The village of Booker is situated almost halfway between Lane End and West Wycombe. In the 13th century it was known as the tithing of Bokar and Booker Common is at least 900 years old. The Dashwood family of West Wycombe has held the estate for almost 300 years.

Many changes have taken place in recent years. Housing estates and new roads have replaced fields and hedgerows. Old maps show a brickfield and two isolation hospitals. One of these is now Booker Hospital and the other a residential home for the elderly called Beechlands.

It is said that in the 1920s, Mr Chadwick, the High Wycombe Sanitary Inspector, had the task of transporting infectious patients to the hospital. One day in Cressex Lane the floor of the conveyance collapsed, leaving the patients to walk the rest of the way, still inside the ambulance!

Under the presidency of Mr Allan Duggin, Booker Common and Woods Society was formed in 1982 and many improvements have been made.

It is pleasing to know that wild flowers are to be planted by the Society. In former times daffodils and many other wild flowers grew in the fields and hedgerows and they have now disappeared or become very rare.

Despite the adjacent motorway Booker has made determined efforts to maintain its identity.

# Bovingdon Green

Bovingdon Green has a gentle village atmosphere and most of the people who live on the Green find that there is a friendly way of life. This friendship is helped by the fact that in 1968 a group of residents decided to form the Bovingdon Green Preservation Society. This society not only keeps the grass cut and the green looking tidy, but also has social and fund raising activities, a picnic barbecue lunch in the summer and a supper usually twice a year in the Village Hall. Since the society was founded, it has become the custom to plant ornamental trees to the memory of residents who have died.

The Village Hall, built in 1926, is thriving at the present time, being used regularly by many groups in the evening and a successful play group meets every morning during term-time. Bovingdon Green W.I. have met there since it was built and Marlow Common also use the hall.

In 1983 the Lord of the Manor offered Bovingdon Green for sale. It was purchased by a local business man. Life goes on much the same except that the Green now has large notices warning people not to park cars or ride horses.

At one time there was a village school at Bovingdon Green. It was founded by General Sir George Higginson in memory of his wife. This school closed in 1925 and the building was demolished.

For a long time the village supported two public houses. The Jolly Cricketers closed during the 1930s, but the Royal Oak continues and is situated by the pond where mallards raise ducklings every spring.

# Bow Brickhill

'Little Brickhill, Great Brickhill,
Brickhill with a Bow
These three Brickhills
Stand all in a row.'

As this old rhyme explains, our village straddles a steep hillside and sprawls along three lower roads. At the eastern end, All Saints Church dominates the top of the hill. A mile away westwards, and 500 feet below, a tiny railway halt ends the main road through the village. The railway, between Bedford and Bletchley, opened in 1846 and brought employment for many villagers. Names on ancient maps – Sheep Lane, Hogstye End, Back Woods, Blind Pond Field, depict a mainly rural area. Other employment was in the extensive woodlands bordering the church and owned by the Duke of Bedford. Nowadays areas of these woodlands have been cleared and are used for golf, including important events such as the Dunhill Masters.

Dick Turpin is supposed to have galloped in the area, and an old legend tells of a phantom horse near the river, in the valley. Another colourful legend involves the Blind Pond on the north side of the village. As children we were told a richly-jewelled lady with coach-and-four had galloped down to the pond, and such were the depths she was still travelling downwards! It certainly ensured we children never ventured near the pond although we often passed it to walk in the beautiful bluebell woods.

Visitors who brought great pleasure, earlier this century during the summer months, were the Westminster Choir Boys. They came to camp in old railway carriages placed on the south side of the hill. Dr Sidney Nicholson, a village resident who founded the Royal School of Music in 1927, was responsible for these visits. On fine summer evenings we would listen with delight as they sang around their camp fire, the voices floating around the village with a purity of sound not normally heard from the village church choir! An earlier choir was made famous in 1847 when the artist Thomas Webster, staying in nearby Little Brickhill with his sisters, exhibited *A Village Choir* at the Royal Academy. It depicts 16 adults and 5 children singing in the choir gallery (since demolished) of our church and dominated by a central figure conducting the singers and instrumentalists. Descendants of the choir still live in the village. The picture is now in the Victoria and Albert Museum.

The hill is at the end of a greensand escarpment where stone was once quarried for building. An old document exists which confirms permission for 'stone to be dug from these stone pits at 1/6d per yard'. A recent botanical survey of Buckinghamshire churchyards showed ours to be one of the most interesting. This is mainly due to the light sandy soils allowing unusual plants to grow. The lovely wild daffodil is one of the most choice species. It is known locally as the Lent Lily, because, despite the changing date of Easter, it always flowers then. At the bottom of the hill the sands mingle with the stiff clays of the vale.

The Domesday Survey of 1086 records the village as a small rural settlement which the Normans gave to Walter Giffard. 900 years later, while still enjoying rural life, we can savour the technical advantages of an expanding city on our doorstep. Such a promising future built on a rich heritage of the past, augurs well for Bow Brickhill.

# Brill

Brill which is situated some 4 miles north west of Long Crendon is approached from all directions by a hill. It stands some 600 ft above sea level.

A 17th century windmill dominates the common from where there are magnificent views over Aylesbury to Calvert and over Oxfordshire to the Cotswolds. Many years ago the common was quarried, hence the deep undulations. Villagers have the right to graze sheep on this, and in times past refused to have the ground levelled as this would reduce the area of grass.

Cottages are set around a delightful village green. Nearby is the 12th century church with its 15th century tower.

# Burnham

Burnham Hundred, along with those of Stoke and Desborough, make up the Chiltern Hundreds. Burnham has a mention in the Domesday Book. It is no longer a typical English village, though there is still a strong community feeling present. The main street is a conservation area and this will help to preserve the charming appearance of its buildings. Any new building has to be in keeping with the old. Very few of its inhabitants live in the High Street now, so from being a place of bustle day and night it is a busy trading centre during the day and almost deserted in the evenings.

The parish church of St Peter dates from the 13th century, though there is evidence that there was a church on the site before that time. Its structure has seen changes through the years. An extension is being erected at present, the Cornerstone Project. It has a team ministry which serves also the churches of Taplow, Hitcham and Dropmore.

Church Street was the centre of the village and the governing body, the Vestry, was responsible for civil and church affairs until the formation of the Parish Council in the mid 1880s. There was a market hall, stocks and the penitentiary 'Cage' for wrongdoers, the Five Bells, the Bricklayers' Arms, shops and cottages. South of the church the workhouse was built in 1763 but after 80 years it was closed and a primary school was built on the site. This has now disappeared, and a modern house built with the old materials. On the left side of the street there is a Tudor cottage, once a shop, now a private house, in which Mrs Sheila Critchley lived until her death. She began a Dollmakers' Circle in the district and was well known by many associations for her entertaining talks.

South east of the village was a watermill, Haymill. The pond serving it has largely disappeared. There are some large estates on the outskirts. Britwell Court, built in the 14th century, housed a very fine library when owned by the Christie-Miller family. The house was sold to a community of nuns, Servants of Christ, in 1919 and called the House of Prayer. It is no longer a religious house. In 1903 a merchant banker, E. Clifton-Brown, bought an adjoining estate, Burnham Grove, and became famous for his Hampshire Down sheep and Tamworth pigs. This is now the Burnham Beeches Hotel. A previous owner was the uncle of

Thomas Gray, the poet. Dorneywood House is the second home of the Foreign Secretary, having been given to the nation by the late Lord Courtauld Thomson, brother-in-law of Kenneth Grahame, author of *The Wind in the Willows*. Lord Thomson also gave land to the Scout Movement for a permanent camp site.

The forest of Burnham Beeches, about 500 acres, is owned by the Corporation of the City of London. There are medieval remains, Hardicanute's Moat. A beech tree in this forest is thought to be the largest beech butt in England. It is aptly named 'His Majesty' and has a girth, at 3 ft from the ground, of 29 ft 1½ inches. The beech trees form very peculiar shapes as they have been pollarded for hundreds of years for fuel.

# Cadmore End 🐏

Cadmore End is a small quiet hamlet between Lane End and Stokenchurch. Unfortunately when the M40 motorway was built it divided the village into two, but this does not seem to detract from the beauty around it.

As Cadmore End is conveniently situated to Heathrow Airport via the M4 Motorway, we have our share of pilots living here. Most families work very locally or commute to London by train from High Wycombe.

There are many walks nearby including the old 'woolpack track' to Hambleden and the Thames and we get people taking the 'walks from the car' at weekends.

The Smock windmill which has been restored and used as a 'cottage' can be seen over the trees from this track. This was used in the film *Chitty Chitty Bang Bang*.

There are old brickworks on one side of Cadmore Common but they have now been disused for many years.

The social life revolves around the village green cricket club, The Blue Flag and The Ship public houses, the church and school.

# Castlethorpe 🐏

Castlethorpe is one of the most northern villages of Buckingham-shire. It is bounded in the west by the river Tove which separates it from the Northamptonshire village of Cosgrove. It is intersected by the main railway line between London and the north of England. At one time Castlethorpe was part of Hanslope and a large and impressive earthwork of the motte and bailey castle is reputed to be Hanslope Castle. The castle was the seat of the Manduit family and has had a chequered career.

The church of St Simon and St Jude stands within the fortifications of the castle and parts of the church date back to Norman times. Over the centuries considerable alterations have taken place within the church. At one time there was a west gallery in the church which was known by the congregation as the 'fishes pew'. It was occupied by the Eel, the Pike and the Whiting families.

In 1905 a spark from a passing train set fire to houses in North Street having 'jumped over' the houses in South Street. The women and children were given hospitality by neighbours and the men were allocated the waiting room in the railway station. This was the second spark since the turn of the century to cause fire in the village. Most of the menfolk worked either in Wolverton railway works or on the land, but as the century has moved on so have the occupations. In spite of the fact that the railway station was closed in the 1960s Castlethorpe is now quite a 'commuter village'. Farming still plays a large part in the village life.

Our station may have closed but Castlethorpe has not gone to sleep.

# Chalfont St Giles 🌿

Chalfont St Giles lies about a quarter of a mile from the A413 about three miles south east of Amersham. This distance from the main road has helped to preserve its identity as a village with church, pond and village green surrounded by cottages. It has a recorded Roman road running through it, so has nearly 2,000 years of history. It is, in fact, a fine example of the development of an English village through the ages.

The church was built in Norman times and the dedication to St Giles may possibly refer to the beechwoods that once covered the surrounding hills, St Giles being the patron saint of woodlands as well as the sick, poor, lepers and cripples. The east window of the church is said to have been damaged by Cromwell's cannon stationed in Stone Meadow while Cromwell himself was lodged at Stone House. The river Misbourne flows through Stone Meadow and local folklore has it that if it stops flowing it foretells disaster.

The principal great house of St Giles is The Vache, a very ancient manor house. The de la Vache's, the owners of the manor may well have brought the name with them from Normandy when they came to England with William the Conqueror and took possession of the estate. The property passed later to Thomas Fleetwood, Master of the Mint to Queen Elizabeth I, and was held by that family until George Fleetwood, one of the judges of Charles I, was evicted from the property after the Restoration in 1660. The Vache estate is now owned and occupied by the British Coal Board.

Between St Giles and St Peters on the north side of the Misbourne valley is another great house, Newlands Park. It was constructed by a Georgian banker, Abraham Newlands, who eventually became Chief Cashier of the Bank of England. At that time all bank notes were signed by hand and since Mr Newland's signature appeared on £5 notes they were popularly known as 'Newlands'.

Chalfont St Giles is principally known for Milton's cottage, although it was never owned by him. When the Plague came to London in 1665 John Milton asked his friend and former pupil, Thomas Ellwood to find him a refuge. Ellwood rented the cottage on Milton's behalf but could not be on hand to welcome Milton and his family to the cottage because he was in prison for being a Quaker. He was released from prison while Milton was still at the cottage and visited him there. Milton is said to have handed him the manuscript of *Paradise Lost* which he had just completed, asking for his opinion. On returning the manuscript Ellwood said 'Thou has said much here about Paradise lost, but what has thou to say of Paradise found?' Legend relates that after the Plague Milton returned to London and wrote *Paradise Regained*. The cottage is now the only existing building in which Milton is known to have lived. It was purchased by public subscription in 1887 in honour of Queen Victoria's Jubilee, the Queen heading the list with a donation of £20.

On the hillside above Chalfont St Giles is an obelisk some 60 feet high made of flintstones with the corners strengthened with brick. Although the obelisk itself gives no clue as to why it is there, local legend has it that at this spot King George III, being out hunting and separated from his attendants by a sudden fog, accosted a yokel and asked where he was. The yokel replied that 'Peters is down there and Giles over yonder but this 'ere ain't rightly a place at all'. To which the King replied 'we will make it a place then'. He had the obelisk erected to mark the spot.

# Chalfont St Peter

Chalfont St Peter is a village and parish on the main road, A413, from London to Aylesbury. It lies in a valley on the spur of the Chiltern Hills. The river Misbourne runs through the middle of the main village street, now culverted in the shopping area.

This was an agricultural area, but much has changed since the population exploded. This grew tenfold in 100 years from 1,456 in 1881 to 14,498 in 1981, the latest census year, and certainly much more by 1986.

The village street was very pretty, with some early 16th century buildings of rare and distinctive architecture. These included two very rare brick-built, half-timbered cottages which we called Wingfields.

The parish church of St Peter, in the diocese of Oxford, stands in the centre with the churchyard flanking the road. The church is a red brick and stone building with a fine tower. The present building was re-erected in 1708, the previous one having collapsed.

The Greyhound Inn, a striking red-brick building, had an imposing coach entrance. Sadly, this has been infilled of recent years. This was a stop for the stage coaches in the 18th and early 19th centuries. The infamous Judge Jeffreys held court here when he lived at The Grange, a short distance away.

The George Inn, a cream washed building, stands facing the parish church. This still retains its coach entrance. A notice over a low door states: 'Duck or Grouse'! Alongside the inn a large modern shopping centre, with car park, has risen from the ruins of the 16th century 'Barrack Yard'.

The Grange is a charming house, built on the site of a former imposing residence and is steeped in history. Here was once the home of the infamous Judge Jeffreys and is now the Holy Cross Convent, a boarding and day school for girls.

The Cottage Hospital, its early title, was built in 1871 and was the gift of the Hibberts of Chalfont Park, with initially six beds and one cot. Now there are over 30 beds and, through the generosity of the public, outpatients and physiotherapy departments, a new X-ray department, day rooms and many other amenities have been added. It is now named The Chalfonts and Gerrards Cross Hospital and serves several parishes.

# Chearsley

Chearsley is a small village of less than 500 inhabitants. The unknowing traveller can easily miss its charms as very little of the village is on view from the main road. The detour down the side of the hill, with the winding, hollow lanes, is worth taking.

The village probably developed from a collection of small scattered farmsteads which, by the 9th century, was known as 'Ceored's leah'. By the time of the Domesday survey in 1086, there may have been about 50 inhabitants. Later, the village developed on the north and east side of the church, and the remains of a medieval moat can be seen in the field between the church and the river Thame.

Many of the cottages are thatched, and if a walk is taken down School Lane, there is an old terrace of cottages, which used to house the lace makers of yesteryear. If the electricity wires are ignored, one can almost see the ladies, with their straw pillows and bobbins, sitting outside the cottages, making their beautiful Buckinghamshire lace patterns. This is also the spot where the ratcatcher used to frighten the girls coming out of school! He would save the little white mice he had caught and place them under his hat. On seeing the schoolgirls, he would raise the hat in true gentlemanly fashion, and the mice would cascade to the ground!

In the Conservation area, Watts Green is particularly picturesque, with its mixture of thatched, timber and witchert dwellings. This was once the 'tradesmen's' section of the village, with a shop, ale-house, cobbler's shop and nail-makers shed in close proximity to each other, around the green. The nail-maker's shed can still be seen in the garden of 'Needlemakers' cottage, but, sadly, the matching cobbler's shed on the other side of the lane was destroyed.

At the bottom of the hill, stands the 12th/13th century church.

This little building with its simple white interior, is much loved by all who visit.

Near the church, is a spring which trickles into a pond, known as Stockwell. It is suspected that this is the holy well to which pilgrims made homage in previous centuries. Chearsley has many springs and often water can be heard running through the road drains in the driest of weather. Stockwell was still running in the famous drought of 1976.

# Cheddington 🐝

Cheddington of the early 1920s was a very different village from that of today. Then it was a very rural community comprised of not more than 200 houses. The largest of these were the Rectory, Manor House, White House and the farms. There were very few detached houses and the rest were terraced cottages. The 3 pubs at present in the village were supplemented by The Old Inn where beer only was sold.

The village then boasted 2 general shops which stocked everything from peanuts to glass lamp shades (for the oil lamps then used), a bakery with daily deliveries, butcher, cobbler, drapers, post office, newspapers, coal merchant, forge and 2 farmers delivering milk, builders and 2 undertakers. In addition to grocers from Tring and Leighton Buzzard who delivered orders and butchers from Long Marston and Ivinghoe, there was also a fishman and an ice cream seller from Wing.

The local men were mostly employed on the farms, with local builders, on the nearby Rosebery estate or on the railway. Cheddington was and still is the only village on the main Euston line. It is believed we had this honour because of the convenience for taking Lord Rosebery's racing horses to Newmarket or wherever they were running. The railway employed a staff of about 20 on the station alone. Besides plate layers, there was even a gasometer to supply gas for lighting the station and the station master's house. There was also a branch line to Aylesbury. The drivers knew all the passengers and checked we were all there every morning, if not they looked out for us rushing up late and would stop the train and hoist us up to the carriage. The train was liable to delays when cattle strayed on the line and had to be driven off.

The women in Cheddington went to work in the factories at Apsley and Berkhamsted, and those at home often did plaiting for the famous Luton straw hats, did dressmaking or made the Bucks lace.

Practically every house had a garden or allotment and very few people ever bought vegetables. But above all Cheddington produced plums. Nearly all the new estates are built on old orchards. Greengages, Victorias, damsons, Pond's Seedlings, Early Rivers, but above all prune damsons which were used in plum and apple jam and for dyes. They are not a dessert variety and very few remain except in gardens. They were sent to Covent Garden and Spitalfields market for sale, and in a good year one ton a day would be packed in the round skips sent by the fruit firms and collected daily by Tommy Lambourne on the coal cart and sent to London for sale along with the churns of milk the farmers sent to the London dairies.

Cheddington became famous in 1962 because of the Great Train Robbery which happened at a railway bridge just outside the village. A record sum of two and a half million pounds in used bank notes were taken and at the trial of the robbers record sentences of 30 years in prison were inflicted by the Assize Judge at Aylesbury.

# Chenies

The village of Chenies is mainly situated on a hill above the beautiful valley of the river Chess.

Its history is a long one, dating back to Saxon times when it is believed that there was a wooden church on the site of the present St Michael's church. The name Chenies is thought to derive from Cheney; a family of that name once being the Lords of the Manor.

In 1526 John Russell married the heiress to the Cheney estate and became the village's most notable personality. The owner of a small Dorset estate and a gifted linguist he had the good fortune to be presented to Henry VII, who made him a gentleman usher – the first step to an earldom and the great Bedford fortune. Under Henry VIII John Russell became Lord High Admiral of England and he served both Edward VI and Queen Mary Tudor as Lord Privy Seal. It is said that his portrait shows a man who was cautious, prudent and thoughtful and this he must indeed have been to serve four Tudor monarchs and to die peacefully in his bed!

John Russell loved the village. He enlarged the manor so that he could entertain Henry VIII and he expressed the wish to be buried in the village church. This his widow arranged and built the Chapel in which all the subsequent Earls and Dukes have been buried up to the present time.

At the same time that the manor was enlarged the village also grew and became considerably bigger than it is today, though there are still several timber-framed cottages dating from this period.

A later and quite different personality, whose memory is still treasured in the village was the Rev Lord Wriothesley Russell, a younger son of the 6th Duke of Bedford. He came to be Rector of Chenies in 1829, when he was 25 years old and stayed until his death in 1886. Although offered high office in the Church he refused to leave his village flock. In the days before the school was built he taught the village children to read and write in the Rectory kitchen and it is recorded that he refused to have a new carpet in his study as the men would not like to walk on it in their boots. The affection in which he was held is attested to by the lovely illuminated address, with its charming watercolour scenes, which still hangs in the church. This address was presented to the Rector by the villagers to mark his 50th anniversary as their priest. On each side of the address may be seen the signatures of the donors — said to include the whole village. It is interesting that some of these names are still to be found either in the village or the surrounding area.

Life in the village must have continued with little change for many years. The men worked on the estate farms and woodlands. Dodd's Mill, at one time a paper mill, functioned as a corn mill until 50 years or so ago and watercress was and is still grown in spring water near the Chess. The larger houses in the area provided work for both men and women. The village blacksmith shod horses and repaired farm machinery. Bread was baked locally and the necessities of life could be bought in the village shops. With mechanisation, however, came change. Young people were forced to seek employment in nearby towns. Buses and cars took people to more urban areas to shop at more competitive prices and so the local shops closed, the last being the post office in 1975.

In 1954 the Duke of Bedford sold his Chenies estate in order to pay death duties, bringing to a close the Russell family's long tenure of the estate. However, the split between Woburn, the seat of the Russell family and Chenies is not complete. The family still show an interest in the affairs of the village and it is still in the Bedford Chapel in St Michael's church that the Dukes are laid to rest among their ancestors.

# Chesham Bois ✿

The earliest that is known about Chesham Bois is that a prehistoric trade route came down from Ley Hill, across the river Chess and up Hollow Way Lane, continuing to Amersham, Penn and eventually the south coast. Ancient tracks such as this were marked at frequent intervals by stone boulders and locally the distinctive puddingstone, a mass of pebbles in a stone-like matrix, was used. Many of these stones can still be seen lining the drive from Bois Lane to the church. The Domesday Survey of 1086 records that Chesham included a Saxon manor given by William the Conqueror to his half-brother Odo, Bishop of Bayeux: but in the reign of King John its ownership in fee was acquired by a Norman family named de Bosco or du Bois. William du Bois occupied a manor house which he either rebuilt or erected about 1213, with a family chapel nearby. This forms the chancel of the present parish church of St Leonards, although the house itself has long since disappeared. The church is approached through an avenue of chestnut trees, and is first seen across an open meadow.

The manor passed through a number of different hands until Sir Thomas Cheyne purchased it in 1446. Sir Thomas was a Lollard, of whom there were a number in the Amersham area, and some were burnt at the stake in 1414. Sir Thomas himself was imprisoned in the Tower in the same year for his heretical beliefs. The Cheynes held the manor for the next three centuries until 1738 when it passed to the Russell family, who became Dukes of Bedford. The old rectory on Chesham Bois Common was designed and built in the characteristic Russell style, similar to that used in

Chenies village and at Woburn; the two-storeyed porch bears the date 1833 and displays the ducal coronet.

Two farms were recorded at Chesham Bois in the 16th century, Manor Farm and Bois Farm. The latter is now part of the Beacon School on the main road to Chesham, where a massive and splendidly timbered Elizabethan barn, partly converted into a farm building, can still be seen. For a time in the 1930s this was used as a repertory theatre. Bois Mill, in the Chess valley has a long history. The house occupies the site of the original water-mill recorded in the Domesday Survey, when it was worth three shillings.

Even up to the middle of the 19th century very little development took place in this peaceful part of Bucks. The population in 1806 was 135 and fifty years later it had risen to 258. Towards the end of the century the village around Anne's Corner began to develop and when an enterprising builder, William Gomm, built some of the substantial houses facing the Common, most of their doors, fireplaces, balustrading and window-frames came from the late period houses which had been demolished to make way for Marylebone Station. Most of the present day housing development has taken place since the Second World War, with large gardens being divided up.

# Cholesbury cum St Leonards

A group of four villages comprising Hawridge, Cholesbury, Buckland Common and St Leonards are known as the Hilltop Villages, because they range along the north edge of the Chiltern Hills.

This is designated an area of outstanding natural beauty, and the many beautiful beech woods, planted to supply the chair industry of High Wycombe and brush making in Chesham were used to support the local craft of 'bodging'. Brick making was the other industry, and Matthews still produce hand made bricks. Most of the clay pits have been filled in, as grazing land is in demand for the newest local industry of horse riding. New, timber stable buildings and arena for schooling horses are becoming quite a feature of the landscape.

Village life was different in pre-Second World War times. A resident remembers when she lived in a two room cottage on

Hawridge Common. Every Saturday she walked to Chesham to do errands. Later she cycled to work, as a housemaid and even today some people cycle daily down to Chesham. A bus service started in the 1930s and we still have a limited service, used by the few who have no car. Walking is now a leisure activity, the motor car a necessity. Today all shopping has to be done in the local towns, our post offices and village shops have closed, and tradesmen no longer call, but one feature of village life survives. We have at least fifteen clubs and societies covering a wide range of interests from the Vale of Aylesbury Hunt Pony Club, to football, cricket and seniors clubs. There is a Local History Group and, of course the W.I. Our best natural feature a large common is kept cleared by the Commons Preservation Society, whilst the Drama Group entertains us three times a year.

# Coleshill ✺

Coleshill is a lovely village which is set back from the main road between Beaconsfield and Amersham leaving us free from through traffic. In 1669 Thomas Ellwood, the Quaker leader, wrote these directions to his friend:

> 'Two miles from Beaconsfield, upon the road
> To Amersham, just where the way grows broad,
> A little spot there is called Larkin's Green,
> Where on the bank some fruit trees may be seen;
> In midst of which, on the sinister hand,
> A little cottage covertly doth stand.
> "Soho!" the people out and then enquire
> For Hunger Hill; it lies a little higher.
> But if the people should from home be gone,
> Ride up the bank some twenty paces on,
> And at the orchard end, thou may'st perceive
> Two gates together hung. The nearest leave,
> The furthest take, and straight the hill ascend,
> The path leads to the house where dwells thy friend.'

Larkin's Green is still there to-day, by the Magpies Pub. Ellwood's timber framed house at Hunger Hill, where the Quaker Monthly Meetings were held, was just in Hertfordshire, conveniently out of reach of the Buckinghamshire magistrates who persecuted the Friends. It was replaced by Ongar Hill farm in 1873. Going up Magpie Lane, Bowers Farm lies back on the right, a lovely red brick and timber framed house with the oldest oven in Coleshill, panelled walls, and a cased staircase so that the servants could reach their bedrooms without disturbing the family. Bowers was probably built by George Coleshill in 1614, on the site of the medieval manor of Stockbury.

Passing Old Rafters, The Wattles, and Lawyers Cottage, all old names, you reach the little fork in the road, and the Common. In 1300 it was called Coleshill Green, and later, Donkey Common, as horses and donkeys grazed there. On the other side of the road stands the windmill, which the new owners are restoring to its former full-sailed glory. This is the start of the village centre. The blacksmith's Forge, Fleur-de-Lys pub, and two more cottages formed a row, now converted into Forge House. The Slade family worked this forge for over a century, and in the last generation, seven out of nine sons were blacksmiths. Their family cricket team played the rest of the village, in the middle of the road before we had a cricket meadow!

One of the features of the village is the pond, which used to be called the 'Clenemer' and was then part of the Common. Once a year the gypsies would camp there and hold a fair, watering their horses in the pond. Waggons would be driven through in dry weather to stop the wheels from splitting. One cold winter, Mr Slade made a bet that the pond was solid ice, and drove a team of two horses, (shod with ice studs), and a loaded coal waggon across to prove it. He won his bet!

On round the village is Stock Place, once the manor house, and home of the poet Edmund Waller. He wrote a flattering ode to his relation, Oliver Cromwell, and later another to Charles II at the Restoration. The King complained that his ode was inferior to Cromwell's. Waller replied 'May it please your Majesty, we poets are never so successful in fact as in fiction'. Some of his poetry was said to have been written under an oak tree which gives its name 'Waller's Oak' to a nearby house, and still stands to-day.

The road forks again at Hill Meadow, a group of houses built by the Council, and a little further along is The Rosary (a farm in the 17th century), and the imposing late Georgian facade of Coleshill House, which conceals an earlier 18th century building. Sir Bernard Docker lived here, but now it has been converted to comfortable flats, which command a view to Windsor Castle and the Post Office Tower in London. The original grounds now form the gardens of the houses in Chase Close. Round the corner lies the cricket meadow. The Club is enthusiastically run, with a flourishing club house, and the far side of the pitch is used by an archery club.

More old cottages complete the semi circle back to the main road where the water tower stands, perhaps our best known landmark, which can be seen from miles around. Its small reservoir provides all the water for our village, so that old wells and storage tanks have fallen into disuse.

# Cublington

There cannot be many villages in England that have actually moved, but Cublington has! It is situated in the Vale of Aylesbury and the earliest mention of Cublington is in the Domesday Book when 'Coblincote' consisted of 10 hides (1000 acres) and land for nine ploughs. The property, worth £6 per annum, then belonged to one Gozelin from Brittany, a follower of William the Conqueror.

In 1322, sixteen households in the village were wealthy enough to be taxed but by 1341 when King Edward III imposed new rates on country parishes it was reported that about 100 acres of land lay fallow and uncultivated and 13 houses stood empty. The tenants, being so poor, had left the village. There were few lambs and sheep and no-one substantial enough to be taxed. For what specific reason, it is not clear, maybe the Black Death and badly drained land, but the village went into decline.

By 1400 it had been reborn on its present site with a new church built in its centre. Many of the materials of the old church — stone and timber — were re-used in the new one and some of the fittings, like the old parish chest, were installed in the new church. This old chest — the oldest in Buckinghamshire — is still in use today.

The old village site is still visible after all these years and is classified as an Ancient Monument. It lies in the field at the end of Ridings Way and has a footpath running through it.

Journeying today towards Cublington from Stewkley one travels along a switchback of a route lined on both sides by farmland, tall hedges and verges of wild flowers until one comes upon what remains of the Old Manor and its outbuildings. Built in the early 18th century the Manor House was burned down around 1800 but the granary and range of stables and dovecotes, having stood empty and derelict for many years have now been restored to make two beautiful homes.

Turn here into Reads Lane, named after a local farmer whose family, four generations later, still farm in the village. Tucked away along Reads Lane one finds the beginnings of a very modern farming venture – the production of ewes milk cheese and yoghurt. The lane leads out onto the Wing road.

It is just a short distance to the crossroads and it is along here one finds the village hall. Originally the village school, it was built with money provided by a generous local benefactor, Mr Biggs. It closed as a school many years ago but was re-opened during the Second World War to accommodate the many children who were evacuated to the village.

A few yards further on are the 'Evergreen Nurseries' where so many varieties of conifer are grown. This is the site of the village bakehouse which closed about 25 years ago. A certain Mr Stonal made pies locally which were cooked at the bakehouse before being sold out of the area.

At the crossroads, obscured by a high hedge is the village pond. Before water was piped to the village women were known to have used the water from the pond for their washing. In those days, few houses even had sinks and pumps were used for drinking water. An elderly inhabitant believes there are 22 wells in Cublington, most of which are covered by concrete slabs and a potential hazard for the unwary.

Times have changed considerably since the turn of the century. The mothers were kept busy with their large families whilst their menfolk worked locally on the farms. Young women usually went 'into service', often to other villages or Leighton Buzzard and almost all walked to their places of work. The village was pretty self-sufficient with its own bakery, farm produce and a store but should one have needed to visit Leighton Buzzard, a carrier came twice each week to take passengers. There was poverty and hard work but a strong sense of unity and friendship.

One of the highlights of the year in those days was the Annual Feast with much eating and drinking and jollity. There were amusements for all ages and a wonderful day was enjoyed by all. Efforts were made during the last decade or so to hold a Feast again and for a number of years it was very successful but it no longer takes place.

Described by one elderly inhabitant as 'a rather sleepy village when he was young', Cublington could still be so described today but that, of course, is its charm.

# Cuddington 🐝

Cuddington, a small village of approximately 600 inhabitants, is situated six miles from the County town of Aylesbury.

Cuddington's parish church with its Norman pillars has a list of vicars dating back to the 12th century, and the village also has a Methodist and a Baptist church.

Cuddington, however, is by no means without its own amenities; it has a village store with post office, a hairdresser's, two picturesque pubs and a playing field with club. A well-run village hall is the venue for many weekly activities. All groups in the village combine to organise an annual fete – always a very happy and successful occasion.

There are still a few farms in the parish, but most people work in the surrounding towns, with a few commuting to London. The village also has an increasing number of retired people.

In 1985 Cuddington won the Wilkinson Sword for the Best Kept of all Buckinghamshire Villages. The well looked after churchyard with War Memorial and the two village greens were particularly praised. The Parish Council has an extensive tree planting scheme in hand to compensate for lost elm trees.

One side of the village has a view of the distant Chilterns, whereas a drive way in the centre of the village leads down in the opposite direction to the neighbouring village of Nether Winchendon, whose Manor House estate used to own many of the houses in Cuddington. A narrow stretch of the river Thame runs through the meadows between these two villages, and beyond, the land rises to the ridge of Upper Winchendon.

In 1970 a member of the Cuddington Women's Institute, a

life-long inhabitant of the village with a deep love of the countryside, planned for her fellow members to walk to view the sunrise from the ridge by the Upper Winchendon Observatory.

This dawn walk was so much appreciated that it was repeated the next year, and the next – and soon not only W.I. members but other inhabitants were enquiring when the next walk was to be. Each year Mrs Small chooses the route and then leads an ever-increasing number of early risers.

One Cuddington inhabitant, who speaks very appreciatively of Mrs Small's deep knowledge of the countryside, is a man widely known for his work in helping to make the countryside accessible to all; Tom Stephenson, author of *The Pennine Way*.

Cuddington's dawn walk is a very humble one compared with those made possible by Mr Stephenson, but it is surely fitting that this village should be encouraged to take notice of the surrounding countryside, for we are very proud to have in our midst one who has been praised for his 'long, distinguished and dedicated service in promoting the cause of access to the countryside, and in enhancing the nation's appreciation of it'.

# Dadford

Dadford is a very small village, surrounded by large areas of farmland. To the north we have the famous Silverstone Motor Racing Circuit which has approximately 2/3rds of its area in Bucks and was the the R.A.F. home for Wellingtons in the Second World War.

The well known public school of Stowe is on our doorstep. Set in the lovely grounds, landscaped originally by Capability Brown, it was the home for former Dukes of Buckingham and rumour has it that one Duke decided the village of Dadford should be moved from Stowe to its present position, but the church had to remain in the grounds and so we became part of the parish of Stowe and our church is still there. There are no shops in the village nor do we have a pub, but our Village hall was the old village school and the building was given to the village by the Close-Smith family who for many years owned Boycott Manor.

At the end of the picturesque Stowe Avenue leading out of Buckingham is the small hamlet of Chackmore. As the church is at

Radclive the parish becomes Radclive and Chackmore. Chackmore itself, like Dadford, has not expanded very quickly but it does boast a pub. The old school was purchased a few years ago and is now the Parish Hall. The Annual Horticultural Show is an event of long tradition, but moved a few years ago from the centre of the village to a site near the Corinthian Arch at Stowe.

Dadford and the surrounding area may be an ideal sleepy location often dreamed about by townsfolk and it is to be hoped that the rolling countryside may continue to survive amongst the increasing demands of the enormous concrete city of Milton Keynes not very far away.

# Denham 🌿

Since earliest times Denham has been owned or visited by many famous people. Connected for centuries to Westminster Abbey, Denham played host to visiting abbots and later, when ancient Savay Farm became a convalescent home for nuns, it is pleasant to imagine the nuns sporting themselves beside the river as their health improved.

At the Dissolution of the Monasteries, Denham was leased to Sir Edmund Peckham, Master of the Mint to Henry VIII, and his son, Sir George, is believed to have entertained Queen Elizabeth I at Denham. If so, Sir George must have overspent on his entertaining, because his estates were seized by the Crown in 1596 for debt, and leased to Sir William Bowyer.

Great Royalists, the Bowyer family lost their fortunes during the Civil War and sold the Manor of Denham to Sir Roger Hill, who built the lovely Denham Place, at a cost of £5,591.16.9d., between 1688 and 1701. Very little changed since 1770, Denham Place has recently received a million pound face-lift by the Sheraton Hotel Management Corporation.

While Denham Place was being built for him, Sir Roger Hill lived in Hill's House, a beautiful mid-17th century red-brick house with Dutch gables, situated in the village street, close to the church. Hill's House is now owned by Sir John Mills, the famous film actor, who can be seen on his doorstep every Village Fayre Day, presiding over his popular Bottle Stall.

In 1250 a charter for a weekly market and an annual fair was granted to the Lord of the Manor. The annual fair continues to this day and every year we enjoy stalls, bands, punch and judy shows, bouncy castles and roundabouts on the Village Green, presented to the inhabitants of Denham by Herbert Ward in 1952, and refresh ourselves at the three excellent old pubs grouped around the Green.

A quarter of an hour's stroll from the village green, back along the Pyghtle, takes a visitor to the oldest building in Denham – Savay Farm. Built on the site of the original Manor House, the farm was fortified and once surrounded by a moat.

Originally a great hall built on Sarsen stones with many very ancient timbers, Savay Farm has been added to over the centuries. At one time Savay Farm was a common lodging house, charging 4d. a night without supper and 6d. a night with supper, and the present owner possesses a notice board requesting lodgers not to wear their boots in bed. During his Black shirt days, Savay Farm was owned by Sir Oswald Mosley.

Not all of Denham is ancient. Close to Savay Farm lies our 'village within a village' the Garden Village of the Licensed Victuallers, of beautifully laid out retirement homes for ex-publicans. Once a year, each July, the Homes hold a garden party and become a mecca for beautifully dressed ladies and their escorts to enjoy their reunions. A few years ago the Duke of Edinburgh opened the garden party by driving in an open carriage through the streets of Denham.

# Dorney

In the very south of the county lies the village of Dorney, bounded by the river Thames, which used to flood the surrounding farmlands, turing it into an island. The manor of Dorney is named in the Domesday Book and was famous for its honey – hence the derivation of its name from the Saxon 'Island of Bees'.

Dorney is three miles from Eton, and approaching from that direction you must first cross Dorney Common, carefully avoiding the cows, whose grazing rights go back to feudal times. The Common is now enclosed by cattle grids, but in the 1920s there were gates, opened for passing traffic by Mr Tugwood, resplendent in a cutaway coat and gaiters. He received a small wage, but made it clear that tips were welcome. There is a tradition that Queen Victoria's carriage once became stuck in a deep pool known as Lot's Hole, and she had to shelter in a cottage.

At the end of the village street is the main entrance to Dorney Court, the beautifully-preserved Tudor manor house, opened to the public in 1981, which receives visitors from all over the world. There has been a house here since before the Conquest, and the present building dates from 1510. It was acquired by Sir James Palmer in 1600, and handed down from father to son ever since. The Great Hall, where the Manor Court was held, contains portraits of twelve generations. Sir James was Chancellor of the Garter to Charles I, and his son Sir Philip was a Colonel in the Royalist army, and cupbearer to Charles II. Philip's brother Roger was the husband of the notorious Lady Barbara Palmer, Countess of Castlemaine, the favourite of the King.

One of the bedrooms at Dorney Court was said to be haunted by a 'Grey Lady', but she has since been exorcised and is seen no more. Today the family still farm the surrounding area, and have developed a new breed of sheep.

Behind the house stands the parish church of St James the Less with its red brick tower. The church is 13th century, but traces of an earlier Saxon window and door can be seen. The large vicarage nearby is now used by the Eton-Dorney Project, begun when the popular Roger Royle was vicar, to provide holidays for under-privileged children, with Eton boys and local people as helpers.

Across the motorway, a winding old road leads to Huntercombe Manor and Burnham Abbey, both ancient sites still in use today. The nuns were turned out of the Abbey by Henry VIII, but the building survived and was re-consecrated in 1915 to become the home of an Anglican order. The farmhouse of the Abbey became a private house named The Chauntry, and was the scene of a horrifying murder in 1853. The owner came home one night to find bloodstains in the hall and the mangled remains of his housekeeper upstairs. She had been battered to death by the groom, Hatto, after a disagreement, and the murderer was duly tried and hanged. Not surprisingly, this house is also said to be haunted.

The old road, known as Marsh Lane, winds the other way towards Dorney Reach. One of the bends, called Climo's Corner, was the site of the forge where the village blacksmith carried on his trade. At Dorney Reach many new houses were built this century leading down to a beautiful stretch of the river. The school and Village Hall are the centre of activity here.

The building of the M4 brought this area with a jolt into the second half of the 20th century, but has made it an attractive base for television personalities and many commuters to London. As the traffic roars past, how many travellers realise the wealth of history hidden among the leafy lanes of Dorney?

# Downley

Green fields, cart tracks and beech trees, that was Downley in the old days, long before new roads and housing estates took over. A cart track past Kiln Pond led from the village through the woods down a sunken lane to West Wycombe at the Pedestal. The local burial ground was on the hill at the church of St Lawrence and so funeral processions would make their way down this bumpy track, the coffins sometimes being carried, should they fall off the cart.

The other way from the village was down Plomer Hill down the Pitch to join up with West Wycombe Road and so on to

Wycombe for shopping. There were no buses until 1927. In 1928, a Mr Holland of the Pioneer Bus Company ran the first bus service. The bus waited at the Pond, opposite where the Downley Donkey now stands, until all the regular customers arrived. One bus left High Wycombe for Downley at mid-day and returned at 12.50 p.m. so that people who worked at Frogmore could go home for dinner, there being no canteens in those days.

There is a cottage in Littleworth Road called Peter's Cottage, named after Peter Smith; his father was nicknamed Jimmy Two-bits. Tradition has it that he acquired this name when sitting over the fire one Sunday morning watching the dinner cooking. His wife called to him and said 'How's the meat cooking?' He lifted the lid and replied 'Which bit?' His wife told him that there was only one bit, but James said 'No, there's two!' On inspection it turned out that a frog had been put in with the water from the well!

Mr Dicky Gray was one of the village characters, with his long grey beard, a sacking apron tied round his middle with a piece of string and a cap with ear flaps stuck on his head. His string of donkeys would plod behind him as he set off down Plomer Green Lane shouting out 'Whoa Parker, hurry along Jenny'.

The Common was widely used; horses, sheep, goats grazed there and sometimes geese.

In the middle of the village there was a furniture factory built of wood and owned by Mr Bridgewater Spriggs. Mines and West's offices now stand on that site. Most of the timber was brought from the saw mills in High Wycombe by horse and cart, but the first commercial motor transport in Downley was a motor-cycle and side-car.

There have been many changes in Downley since those days. Only a part of Downley Village remains unchanged. The rest is joined up with High Wycombe. We have still the Memorial Hall which serves many organisations but now we have also the Church Hall and the Pastures Methodist Hall.

St James Church serves both the Church of England and the Church of Rome. There are Methodist Chapels on Sunny Bank and in the Pastures. There is also a Baptist Chapel.

There are many organisations to cater for different tastes and meet the demands of young and old.

Fortunately the furniture industry continues to thrive and Mines and West specialise in hand made furniture.

# Drayton Parslow

Before the Second World War, Drayton Parslow had a population of about 300, electricity but no mains water, no main sewer, or street lighting. There was a small shop, a post office and two pubs.

Apart from the half-dozen farms in the parish there were a number of smallholdings and most families had one or more allotments on which they not only grew vegetables but also kept hens. The main sources of employment were agriculture, the brick-works at Newton Longville and the railway at Bletchley.

The biggest landowner was Lord Carrington who allowed a piece of land to be used as a recreation ground which in the summer was home to a thriving and successful cricket team.

Today the population of Drayton Parslow has risen to about 400 and it is still growing. Because of its proximity to Milton Keynes many of the residents work there and some commute to London daily.

On the outskirts of the village is an assortment of buildings which are rapidly becoming derelict. It was known for many years as 'The Camp' and was erected during the Second World War as an extension of the now famous Bletchley Park. It has been altered and extended over the years and used as a prisoner-of-war camp, a hostel for displaced persons working at the brickyard, and Admiralty medical records office and finally a residential training college for Post Office and British Telecom engineers. Drayton Parslow has never had a resident squire and a former villager once remarked that 'every man was his own gaffer' and this is as true today as it was then!

# East Claydon
# & Botolph Claydon

Claydon House, about seven miles South of the town of Buckingham, had four villages which grew up around it, owned by the Estate, and housing its workers and those traditional craftsmen whose skills were needed to support a farming community. Two of these are the village of East Claydon, and the hamlet of Botolph

47

Claydon. The only church, dedicated to St Mary, dates from the 15th century, and is in East Claydon. Nevertheless, until recent times, Botolph Claydon was always the larger settlement.

A clock tower, built in 1913, joins—or separates – the two parts. It has one face for each community. To the north side of the tower is East Claydon village school. On the south side of the tower is the Village Hall, which, when it was built by the Verney family, also housed a Public library, well-stocked with books at the family's expense.

In the curve of the Winslow Road in East Claydon is New Farm, which, in former times, was a coaching station. The old coaching track can still be walked as a public footpath.

In both villages a number of thatched cottages remains, though only one (in Botolph Claydon) is still unmodernised and owned by the Estate. The process of modernisation has included the joining together of two or three very small dwellings which were under the same roof, so that now one loses the awareness of the cramped conditions in which families had to live.

The original cottages often used to have a fireplace in the backyard for boiling kettles, and cooking in summer weather. Water, of course, came from the pump or from wells, and main drainage did not arrive until the 1960s.

Since the Second World War, the rapid increase in farm mechanisation, and the consequent decrease in numbers of farm workers, has caused the character of these villages to change. Almost all the houses are now privately owned, and are lived in by people who work elsewhere.

Nevertheless, within the memory of people now in their sixties, the farms were worked with horses, and it was a familiar sight to see one tethered to the railings outside the forge in Botolph Claydon or to see wagon- and cart-wheels awaiting repair outside the wheelwright's shop next door. The Wiggins Brothers carried on this joint enterprise. At the weir in Weir Lane (now an overgrown pond full of bullrushes) the hooves of the working horses were cleaned of the clinging clay from which the district gets its name.

# Edlesborough

'What I spent I had,
What I gave I have,
What I refused I am being punished for,
What I kept I have lost.'

So says the unique Rose Brass of Edlesborough church, which stands high on a chalk mound overlooking the Vale of Aylesbury and Ivinghoe Beacon. The mound may or not be an ancient British burial mound, but the view from it is superb.

Below the church is a 16th century tithe barn, which by its size, 180 feet long, shows how flourishing Edlesborough must once have been. Originally thatched, now tiled with mellow peg-tiles, its timber-framed walls in-filled with brick and Totternhoe clunch from the village next-door-but-one, it is being carefully restored to fit its new role as offices. Church Farm, its host, is farmed from outside, and the buildings will be houses. The farm has a spring-fed moat inside which is a dove-cote, and round the moat still rides the ghost of Jack the Leather, 'Old Leather Breeches', a highwayman who was dragged from his hiding place in the farm stables to the gibbet at the Beacon. While in hiding his only exercise had been at night, riding the farm horses round the moat, and the lathered horses were spotted one morning by the soldiers sent to find him.

The moat may have surrounded a monastic building. There is certainly a stew pond and fish trap in the grounds of the school next door, which the children are hoping to restore. Let us hope the ghost enjoys his renovated environment. A few yards further along the road, in the grounds of the Old Vicarage, another ghost, that of a gardener murdered in a brawl between rival households, must hear the sounds of children at play and be reminded of happier times.

The ghost of Dick Turpin only frequents the village at night. He had a secret hide-out at Butler's Manor at Northall, where a now blocked up window once commanded a view of laden stage coaches passing Ivinghoe Beacon. There was plenty of time for him then to ride across country to hold up the coach at the old road at Dunstable. He rides now of a dark night along the narrow road between the church and the Tring Road.

The village green, a large, well-laundered open space with football pitches, cricket table, tennis courts and children's swings was once gated to stop grazing animals escaping. These grazing rights were held by those living in the surrounding cottages. These are still standing behind the newer houses which were built after the Enclosure Act took effect in Edlesborough in 1855. The shape of the old common land can still be seen, since the cottagers were allowed to plant and prune damson trees local to the district on the common to a depth of 40 ft, and forward of this 40 ft the new roads were built. In a good year the damsons, sold for dye-making and sent off from Stanbridgeford Station on the train called the Dunstable Flyer, went far to helping a family through the winter. In the last century Edlesborough was a poor village and fast depopulating, from 1,371 in 1891 to 898 in 1921. There were plenty to make full use of the 864 4lb loaves provided yearly by Rendell's 16th century charity.

The 19th century village was owned largely by the Ashridge Estate. Houses were painted in the Ashridge colour of dark maroon brown with identical wooden fences in front. These were the first things to be changed when houses passed into private ownership, the way that nowadays the council house gains a porch and a new front door. Agriculture for the menfolk was supplemented by the women and children's wages from straw plaiting for the Luton hat industry, and one of the new victorian houses had a room for a plait school above the archway to its stable. In 1895, the new Parish Council consisted of five farmers, one farmer and dealer, one plait merchant, a labourer and a carpenter. Now Manor Farm is the last to be farmed by a farmer living in the village farmhouse surrounded by its buildings. Charity Farm, buildings now houses, has the maladjusted ghost of a farmworker. His threshing floor has been lowered to form a new house level, but he remains at the old height and is only ever half seen.

The mill, perhaps on the site of the one mentioned in the Domesday Book, grinds corn no longer, though its machinery ornaments the sitting room of the elegant house it has become. The Rat and Sparrow Club of 1917, helping the First World War effort, by destroying the vermin which preyed on the food supply faded away, though sparrow pie was still being eaten in the 1940s, the Have-a-Go club, which bought much of the children's play equipment too has gone.

The hamlet of Northall, part of Edlesborough parish, once had its own school which was closed in 1905. The two pubs, The Swan and The Village Green Inn, now called The Northall Inn, are still there. A smithy, where horses were shod and iron household items were repaired closed in the early 1930s, as did the wheelwright, carpenter and undertaker, who used to make his own coffins but hired the carriages from Dunstable. A family baker retired in 1953 and the village shop closed in 1983.

But Edlesborough still has a thriving sense of community; good communications though no industry. There are no famous people among us, our recent claim to notoriety through the Fox rapist is best forgotten, but the school is full again and the village grows and flourishes.

# Ellesborough

Ellesborough is beautiful. The church of St Peter and St Paul, rising on its own hillock from the flat vale of Aylesbury, is set against a backcloth of hills. Beacon Hill and Coombe Hill rise above it. The focal point on the latter, the South African War Memorial, is visible for many miles.

It is a favourite place for locals and the view is breath-taking. From there, Chequers, the country home of Britain's Prime Ministers, can be glimpsed. It is in Ellesborough parish, and many Prime Ministers and visiting notables have attended the church services.

The friendly church ghost is said to be the Rev. Robert Wallis, rector of Ellesborough before the Civil War. He was seen on the path up to the church by the present rector not long ago.

The almhouses opposite the church are set in a colourful garden which is tended by the inhabitants. The building is known as 'Lady Dodd's Cottages'.

Down the steep hill is Ellesborough Manor, which has been a home for retired clergy, their wives and widows since 1950.

At St Peter's Cottage there is an aviary of beautiful white doves and down the first lane off the B4010 Mr Will Thomson breeds and delights in prize-winning pigeons. This lane leads to Springs, a fine house, 16th century with Edwardian additions. Immediately below a sheer drop in the lawn, four springs dramatically form the source of the stream called Bonnybrook.

A chain of ponds follow, the last of these being Ellesborough mill pond. The Mill was burnt down by a tramp in 1937.

Further down the Upper Icknield Way is Butlers Cross. This is the hub of the village. The much used Ellesborough village hall, the Russell Arms (the only public house) and the shop and post office are all here. The village hall, built in 1910 by public subscription, is a hive of activity.

# Emberton

The village of Emberton in north Buckinghamshire lies on the southern edge of the wide, lush water meadows through which the Great Ouse winds. The old coach road from Newport Pagnell used to swing between its fine stone houses and past its clock tower before setting off across the causeway and bridge into Olney.

Today, rescued by a by-pass, the village seems to the casual visitor a quiet and tranquil place, the clock tower still providing the focal point and parts of the ancient high street shaded with magnificent chestnuts, copper beeches and sycamores. But the quiet is deceptive. Though the number of its working farms has dwindled and lace making is now a hobby instead of an industry, Emberton is underneath humming with activity.

From what archaeologists have discovered there has been a settlement at Emberton from Roman times or earlier. The original form of the name was Eanbeorht's Tun, the word 'tun' meaning a farm. So possibly a Saxon of that name after crossing the North Sea, travelled up the Ouse until he found this good defensive position slightly raised above the flood plain of the river. The Norman conqueror divided Ambreton, as it became known at one point, between the Bishop of Coutance and Judith, Countess of Huntingdon and from then on its manor was held by various great local families until it came into the hands of the Tyringhams.

For as long as there have been records the village seems to have remained remarkably stable. Strangely enough the continuity did not come through the big houses but through the cottages. Names of Emberton people well known today such as Lett, Howson, West, Mynard and Lovell go far, far back.

Emberton has always been dominated by farming and remnants of the great ridge and furrow fields that surrounded the village before it was enclosed in 1798–9 can still be seen. The oldest villagers living today can still remember when seven farms employed the local men and when the main street was pitted and potholed with dust rising in clouds as herds of cattle were driven through night and morning.

At the south end of the village on a piece of rising ground stands the church of All Saints. It was built in the second half of the 14th century but considerably restored in Victorian times. The chancel is said to contain the mortal remains of Sir Everard Digby of nearby Gayhurst, famed for his part in the Gunpowder Plot.

It was the Rev Thomas Fry who gave the village its central focus today. Just below the church, where the High Street curves sharply, he built a clock tower in 1846 which he named 'Margaret's Tower' in memory of his second wife (he had three altogether). It replaced an old elm surrounded by a stone wall. The site had traditionally been known as Emberton Cross, indicating that a preaching cross once stood there. Today, the clock still keeps excellent time. The British Legion lay their poppies beneath its war memorial and the more robust members of the community dance round it on New Years Eve.

Probably the most dramatic development in recent times took place in 1964, not in the village itself but on its outskirts. Just before the bridge crosses the Ouse into Olney were fields rich with gravel. When the construction of the MI began, these fields were heavily quarried and left as an eyesore. But two members of Newport Pagnell Rural District Council under whose authority Emberton then came, had a wonderful idea. They turned the scarred landscape into a huge country park with wildlife reserves, reed fringed lakes and open waters for sailing. So successful was Emberton Park that it won a Countryside award.

# Farnham Common
# & Farnham Royal 🐚

Farnham Common lies in the parish of Farnham Royal. It covers an area of some 2½ miles and has a population of approximately 6,000.

Farnham Royal was the main village with its church of St Mary's, shops, cottages and village pump situated in the centre junction of the cross roads. Farnham Common was known as 'Up End', being the common land of the parish where the livestock was grazed at certain times of the year. As this common area became more populated it became known as Farnham Common.

Farnham Common is on the border of Burnham Beeches, the well known Beech Forest owned by the City of London, having been given to the people of London as a place in the country for their recreation and pleasure. In the 1920s it was very common for coach loads of Londoners to come down for the day at weekends having tea at the tea rooms and enjoying the donkey rides.

A few of the large old houses still remain such as Yew Place, Farnham Park (once called The Chase) and Caldicott.

Yew Place was formerly known as The Rectory, part of which dates back to the time of King John. The original farmhouse was given to a coachman in the service of the Earl of Warwick.

The Chase, now known as Farnham Park, was owned by Mr Carr Gomme, a very influential member of the community, being one of the main organisers of fund-raisers for the building of St John's Church. The house passed into the hands of Sir Gomer Berry, later Lord Kemsley, who had the organ dismantled from Farnham Park and gave it to St John's Church. Farnham Park is now the renowned Farnham Park Rehabilitation Centre presently owned by the East Berkshire Health Authority.

Caldicott is a very imposing house situated on the edge of Burnham Beeches and was once owned by Mrs Harvey who gave money for the extension of Farnham Common Village Hall. Caldicott is now a Boys Preparatory School.

A few names of note who have been associated with Farnham Common have been the artist Rex Whistler's mother, who lived in The Small House in Burnham Beeches; J. M. Barrie, the author of *Peter Pan* and Enid Blyton, the children's author. In Burnham Beeches there is a large beech tree under which Mendelssohn used to sit and compose some of his works in 'peaceful splendour'. Joan Hammond, the opera singer, lived in the part of the village known as Egypt. The Moore family live in the village and hold the record of three generations of one family representing Great Britain in the Olympic Games, Major George Moore having competed in 1948, Lieut. Col. John Moore, his son, in 1956, 1960 and 1964 and Lieut. Mark Moore, his grandson, in 1984. Lieut. Col. John Moore received on O.B.E. for his services to skiing.

Although the village has grown so much since its early days it still maintains its community spirit which will hopefully survive despite the encroachment of the towns and changing boundary lines. In this respect there is a very active Farnhams Society and Parish Council who keep an eye on any threatening changes.

# Fingest 🌿

Fingest is a huddle of houses centred around the Norman church with its unusual saddle-back roofed tower. No doubt this community came into being here because of the several springs which are still around, which would have been a convenient supply of water.

The surrounding farm land is basically chalky, but there is both silt and gravel close to the water sources. The poorer tops of the hills are rough pasture or woodland, mainly beech, but in recent times some conifer has been planted.

Fingest Manor of comparatively recent birth, is set on the site of an old abbey. There are stories of tunnels from the abbey to the church and of course ghostly ladies who roam around. The original name of Fingest Manor was Tingehurst which was once the name of the village. At the entrance to the driveway to the house is the old village pound. Stray animals were collected up and put in the pound and no doubt a fine of some sort would have been paid to get them out again.

Apart from the church which is within the Hambleden Valley group of churches, the meeting place in Fingest is the Chequers Inn.

Early in the century it is said that there was a tiny school, run by the incumbent of the church, in what is now the old rectory. Alas no school now, not even a village hall. How times have changed!

# Flackwell Heath 🌿

Flackwell Heath, three miles from High Wycombe, stretching out in a long line of closely built houses on a spur of the Chiltern Hills, is now reputed to be the largest village in England. Yet it wasn't inhabited at all until the end of the 18th century and then by a few hardy folk prepared to scratch a living from the stony soil, and ladle water from the small fresh-water springs that bubbled from the hillside.

In the strips of woodland that surrounded the heathland in those early days grew many wild cherry trees and, on these wild trees the village folk grafted good cherry stock from the famous Kent

Orchards, and from the spindly cherries vast orchards soon grew.

Strange to think that, not so long ago, we had more cherry trees on the heath than inhabitants and that to-day's vast housing estates were once large cherry orchards.

Every cherry-picking season it became a tradition for the men from the Heath to leave their regular jobs in factories and mills and spend several weeks in the orchards harvesting the cherries.

# Forty Green

The tiny hamlet of Forty Green (originally known as 'Faulty Green') lies within the parish of Penn in Chiltern District and in 1875 consisted of only ten houses and the famous inn, The Royal Standard of England.

A building was mentioned on the site of this inn in documents when Penn Church (of Quaker fame) was dedicated in 1213 and was then called the Ship Inn.

When battles were fought in the nearby beechwoods between the Roundheads and the Royalists, the inn became the headquarters of the Royalists and was called The Standard by the soldiers as the building stood on a hill. The story goes that King Charles I hid there. Certainly after the Restoration of the Monarchy in 1660, Charles II gave permission for the inn to be renamed and it is believed it is still the only one in the country bearing the name of The Royal Standard of England.

Forty Green is surrounded on three sides by woods: Corkers Wood – newly planted with pine, Roundhead Wood, and the largest – Hogback Wood is now owned by the National Trust. The woods still show signs of the 'Bodgers' work. The saw pits used by them are now playgrounds for children. In days gone by these beech woods were used to supply timber for the furniture factories of nearby High Wycombe. Muntjac deer and foxes can still be seen in gardens and woods despite being only 23 miles from London. Part of the commuter belt, few residents work on the land and many are retired.

# Frieth ✍

There are only some two hundred houses in our small village. These surround a square of lanes with Frieth Hill forming one side.

The name Frieth is said to have come from a word meaning forest; an aerial view of the village still shows this to be true, for Frieth appears as a patch of open fields and houses cut out from the surrounding woods.

One could say that Frieth is a comparatively new village, as its little Victorian church was built in 1848. The church stands at the top of the hill beside the village green and its best architectural features are its wood carving and stained glass. Most of the woodwork was done by the firm of West and Collier whose factory was in the village and who employed and housed many of the villagers. The firm specialised in making chairs and carved woodwork for churches and cathedrals and its products were sent all over the world. Sadly, the firm closed during the Second World War.

Most of the beautiful stained glass windows in Frieth Church are by Kempe and were the gift of the Cripps family who lived at Parmoor House until 1948. Probably the most well-known member of Lord Parmoor's family was his youngest son, Sir Stafford Cripps, a famous Chancellor of the Exchequer. Lord Parmoor was referred to as The Squire, and the village owes much to his philanthropy. He owned most of the farms in the northern half of Hambleden parish. But that is all in the past. Now the farmland around Frieth is divided into four large units and no farm labourers live in the village itself. Parmoor House is St Katharine's Convent, and a community of Anglican nuns run it as a home for the elderly.

Ours is not a tourist village like Hambleden, Fingest or Turville, nor will you find Frieth in the many publications about the Chilterns, but we have an undefinable something that welds us into a community. Perhaps we have been fortunate that new buildings have come gradually; one can find an example of most building periods here. Frieth has been spared the large housing estates which could have been difficult to assimilate. Also, the majority of people who have moved into the village have done so because they saw a quality in village life they had failed to find elsewhere. The remark often made, and one we like to hear, is that Frieth is a caring friendly village. Half a century ago no Frieth man would have met another without the friendly greeting, 'Ow be on'. Yes, we still say, 'Good-morning' to one another!

# Fulmer

Nestling between two motorways, the M25 and M40, Fulmer is on the surface the epitome of an English village. It has its winding village street flanked by the village shop and post office, the church, the public house, The Black Horse, and the village hall. There is even a village school which takes children up to eight years old. However, the majority of the people who live in the village do not work there. There is one farm given over to sheep and intensive egg and pig production, an equestrian centre which also houses a branch of the Riding for the Disabled Association and the Muschamp Stud where German Trakhener horses are bred and a very successful dressage competition is held every year. There are numerous large mansions in and around the village, but these have mostly been turned into flats or in one case become the laboratories of a pharmaceutical research company.

Much of the social life of the village is organised by the Fulmer Family Social Club. In addition to Fulmer Day in June when there are stalls, entertainments, sports and a carnival procession, they also organise other social activities like a Christmas social and the fireworks on November 5th.

The Black Horse is the only public house in the area. It started life as a building hut when the church was built in 1610 and was used for the local petty sessions as early as 1681. The present building has been standing – or sinking as there are no solid foundations – on the site since the late 18th century with additions in 1926 and 1952.

Considering Fulmer's closeness to London it is extremely lucky to be surrounded by beautiful and varied countryside.

# Granborough 🌾

Granborough was once part of the Manor of Winslow. A windmill stood on the hill in a field still called Mill Knob.

An older resident recalls the village in times past:

Granborough in the days of my youth was a very friendly village, full of people of all ages, some very old. One thing which remains in my mind is the old ladies sitting in the doorways of their cottages, a shawl around them to keep warm and a pillow on their knees, making lace, without spectacles or any other aid.

Most of the present day inhabitants work outside the village, except those who work on farms. We once had a blacksmith, a wheelwright and undertaker, a coal merchant, baker, builder, post office and general store.

I remember that at one time the house known as Granborough Lodge, then the Vicarage, was supposed to be haunted by a vicar who died at Scarborough by drowning. Although I lived there for a number of years I never saw him.

During the war there was a day of fear and excitement when an American plane dropped a bomb in Church Lane which demolished the house of Mr W. Newman, our greengrocer, and damaged a few others.

There are a very few of the old families left now, but lots of newcomers, who we are pleased to say are very friendly and helpful, both in the church and in social life.

# Great Brickhill 🌾

The name of the village is probably derived from a combination of the Celtic 'Bryh' (hill) and the Anglo-Saxon 'Hylle' (hilltop), although evidence has been found of much earlier Roman and Bronze Age settlements. The village is situated on a ridge, lying on a bed of Greensand and Oxford Clay, the highest point being 500 feet. Consequently, it has panoramic views from all sides over the surrounding farms and woodland and, in turn, can be seen from many distant villages.

Religion has played its part in village life, although the Methodist Chapel has been converted into a dwelling-house and the

Baptist Chapel has been demolished. The parish church of St Mary shows evidence of Norman times, although the present building is mainly 15th century with later additions. The fine peal of bells is regularly rung and the organ, which is a very fine specimen, has recently been restored.

The village boasts two well-patronised public houses, the Red Lion and the Duncombe Arms, two shops (one incorporating the post office), seven working farms and, last but not least, a working forge. Houses run the gamut from 14th century thatched cottages, Georgian and Victorian homes, modern semis, right through to ultra-modern houses and bungalows.

The life style of the village has changed greatly in the past fifty years, with the majority of the adult working population now leaving the village for employment. As there is no regular bus service most families find it necessary to own a car, while a fortunate few have two or even three cars in the family. Mothers frequently complain that they have become unpaid chauffeurs for their children!

Historically, our most auspicious visitor appears to have been Oliver Cromwell, who is reputed to have spent some time in Great Brickhill, visiting his troops who rested here for six weeks while marching from Aylesbury to Northampton during the latter part of the Civil War. The rest was evidently just what the troops needed, as two months later the Parliamentarians claimed victory. The barn in which Cromwell stayed was later converted to a dwelling; it is now a listed building and still known as Cromwell's Cottage.

Another visitor of note was Benjamin Disraeli, at the time of his campaign to become an M.P. for Buckinghamshire. He frequently visited the village as a friend of the then Lord of the Manor, Philip Duncombe. The Manor has been in the ownership of the Duncombe family since the mid-1500s and descendants are still living there today, although the original house was destroyed in 1933.

At the present time, Great Brickhill is still a village completely surrounded by open country – whether it will survive as such or whether it will eventually be swallowed up by the Milton Keynes development remains to be seen.

# Great Hampden 🦢

Great Hampden is one of those places where it is said nothing ever happens but once upon a time it did.

Most villages have their Big House, and Great Hampden is no exception. The large dwelling that stands on top of the hill overlooking the valley between the two Hampdens, was once the home of John Hampden, cousin of Oliver Cromwell. A man of great integrity, it was he who took a stand against his king in opposition to the crippling 'Ship Tax', which ultimately triggered the Civil War in England. He died at Thame after being wounded at the Battle of Chalgrove Field. He was brought home to be buried at Great Hampden. His memorial cross stands, like a sentinel, on the road from Prestwood.

The last Earl of Buckinghamshire to live in his ancestral home was, like his ancestor, a much respected man. Affectionately known as 'The Squire', he knew most of the villagers by name. In 1950, it was he who organised the laying of the cricket field, and when he died, his memorial was an extension to the village hall, incorporating committee room, entrance, and pavilion. The much envied, immaculately maintained field, where for generations sons have followed fathers in the team, still provides a venue for them and their families.

A staunch supporter of the cricket team for many years was the Rev. P. Hill. The love of the game was one of his reasons for taking the living, and when he died in 1985 a great sense of loss was felt by the community. Hampden House, once the ancestral home of the Earls of Buckinghamshire, was taken over as a girls school at the outbreak of the Second World War, and it subsequently took on the role of a film studio, the perfect setting for historical dramas, and macabre films.

When a project to re-discover a village pond was taken up, an enthusiastic band of W.I. members and their families hacked away small trees, shrubs and undergrowth and cleared the site of Blakemore Pond. Water is back, plants are growing, frogs abound, and ducks have been seen. The work of maintaining this small oasis will, it is hoped, continue.

The Chiltern woodland integrating the 50 homes that comprise the village of Great Hampden has, over the years, provided timber for the local furniture industry. At one time the 'bodgers' (chair-leg makers, who worked in the woods) worked there and the last man to ply his trade was a local man, Mr Dean.

# Great Horwood 🐚

As early as 792 A.D. there is a reference to '10 dwellings in the wood called Horwudu'.

Our church of St James is of Norman origin being rather special in the fact that the tower is topped by a Norman 'helmet'.

During the Second World War years we have an airfield here and the village would vibrate to the sound of the engines of the Wellingtons warming up for take-off. All the R.A.F. quarters were at the back of the village away from the High Street. When the war ended we were allowed onto the Camp as it was called, to go to the cinema. Children were allowed in if accompanied by an R.A.F. person and we could sit on the floor in front of the chairs for 6d. or sit on a chair for 9d. The week *Tokio Joe* was shown it was packed houses and every time a Jap plane was shot out of the sky, the cheering by R.A.F. personnel and village children alike could be heard in Winslow.

Now the camp is a housing estate. The airfield is still there but is owned by a large consortium of well-known farmers and the fields between the runways are grazing for sheep and beef cattle. Intensive pig and poultry farming is also carried out.

# Great Kingshill 🐚

Great Kingshill is situated high on the Chiltern Hills, approximately 3½ miles from High Wycombe and 1½ miles from Prestwood.

Way back in history when ponds were a means of water supply to the local populace it had two, one of which was hedged and gated, with stone steps leading to the water. This was for domestic use, the other being used to water the cattle and horses. One still remains somewhat diminished in size, off Pipers Lane. Remnants of the past are still in evidence near the cross-roads in the village, where a terraced pit was used for cockfighting. Today it collects water from the nearby roads and is aptly named Cockpit Hole Pond.

In the 19th century the village consisted of a few farmsteads and brick and flint cottages. These delightfully attractive cottages still stand beautifully maintained.

As time passed and the small community grew, so did industry. One of the busiest must have been the village blacksmith. In addition to shoeing horses he made iron hoops which were burnt onto the wooden wheels of waggons and carriages. Iron was used very much in his work generally. The maintenance of the local farm implements was also part of his work. At the opposite end of the village was the carriage builders and wheelwrights, essential to farmers, but equally important, had the task of making saddle-trees for the army horses during the First World War. W. Anderson, General Engineer, was also involved in war work turning shell heads. After the war the business became a garage and is now in the hands of the son and grandson. Industrious ladies of that period would meet at Robin Cottage, a lovely old building still preserved, to practise the delicate art of lace-making.

Although there was a gradual growth in the village over the years, it was not until after the Second World War that development really began to take place. The whole scene began to change as cherry orchards disappeared one by one, and modern progress enabled people to purchase homes in what has now become an exceedingly desirable village in which to live.

A typically English scene is that of cricket being played on the village green. The Club was founded in 1891 or thereabouts, and is enjoyed by local and visiting spectators alike. Football is played with as much enthusiasm by the Senior and Junior Football Clubs during the winter months.

Opposite the village green is the general stores, established by Gerald Free in 1921. Before electricity was easily available, a hundred-candle-power pressure lamp was attached to the corner of the store for the benefit of the customers. Mr Free used a unique sign, that of an Alsatian's head, accompanied by the words 'Alert Service' on his delivery vans which could be seen frequently around the villages.

Surrounded by meadows and woodland, the village is well-balanced and complete.

# Great Linford 🌿

Great Linford village, with its 12th century church and 17th century manor house, is now part of the new city of Milton Keynes, but still retains its village atmosphere.

The original village green remains, also a cricket pitch and several landscaped areas, all linked by the redways (pedestrian and cyclist paths) and bridleways, surrounded by trees, shrubs and great banks of roses.

The village church is of great interest. Apparently there was a chapel at Linford, on this site, in 1151. The church tower is 12th century with various additions and alterations since. The 17th century manor house was formerly owned by the Pritchard family. Sir William was a Lord Mayor of London and he also built the almshouses which are very attractive and now house various offices. The manor is now owned by Milton Keynes Development Association and has been used as an arts centre. Some of the manor out-buildings have been converted into a community work-shop and a hall where various activities and functions take place.

Linford Lodge Hotel and riding stables also remain as part of the original village, now surrounded by new houses, and serve the community as hotel and a centre for young and old to learn to ride on the many paths in the locality.

The canal runs to the north of Great Linford. It is quite widely used by barges, canal buses, the fishermen and busy families of moorhens. The towpaths have been cleared and it is pleasant to walk along them.

It is hard to believe that this lovely village is within a ten minute ride of the biggest indoor shopping centre in England at Milton Keynes.

# Great Missenden 🌿

There has been a village of Great Missenden since Saxon times. The name is derived from the river Miss or Mease and from the word 'dene' – a narrow wooded valley. It is mentioned in the Domesday Book. Today the river is known as The Misbourne and whereas it was once an attractive stream rising near the Black

Horse at Mobwell and serving several watermills, it is now almost non-existent and is enclosed in a culvert beneath Buryfields Recreation Ground.

Situated as it is on the main road between Aylesbury and London, Great Missenden was once a popular stopping place for travellers and at one time there were twelve inns along the High Street.

The large number of inns provided a great deal of employment for the villagers, together with blacksmiths, wheelwrights etc. The many farms in the area also provided work and on the outskirts there was at one time a brickworks. The women of the village were involved in straw-plaiting for the hatmakers of Luton and St Albans, lacemaking and in the service of the gentry who occupied the many great country houses in the area.

The one thing which brought the greatest change to life in Great Missenden was the coming of the Metropolitan Railway in 1892. This meant that trade for the inns was drastically reduced, the need for so many horses and horse-drawn vehicles also fell and thus many of the villagers were forced to seek other employment which was not readily available at that time.

Once the journey to London via the train was made easier, several notable people began to look at Great Missenden as a place to live. Many politicians, actors, authors and businessmen needing to be within easy reach of the capital have found the Chiltern Hills surrounding Great Missenden an ideal place to make their homes.

Important buildings include Missenden Abbey, founded in 1133 by William de Missenden who had inherited the land from Walter Giffard, a knight of the Norman conquest.

The Abbey eventually owned much land in the neighbourhood and in 1367 King Henry III granted a fair to be held on August 14th and 15th – the feast days of the Blessed Virgin to whom the Abbey is dedicated. This fair survived until the middle of the 19th century.

The Parish Church of St Peter and St Paul stands on the site of a Saxon church and although the exact age of the church is not known, the first Vicar was appointed in 1199. In the churchyard, the tomb of Thomas Backhouse commemorates a retired sailor who, in 1800 was buried upright under a pyramid-shaped monument on the hillside above Havenfields. Some years later his body was removed to the churchyard.

In today's Great Missenden the High Street is very different.

Gone are the inns, the small grocery shops, the haberdashers and many others to be replaced by numerous antique dealers, estate agents and a supermarket. The old ironmongery business remains together with the bakery and the butchers. Mr Caleb King, who started the ironmongers shop, could make anything in tin-ware starting from scratch. He also had the first motor car in Great Missenden — an Austin Seven — which could be hired to take fares almost anywhere.

At Havenfields there is a violin maker's establishment where highly skilled work is still carried out.

# Grendon Underwood 🌿

Grendon Underwood lies between the Roman road of Akeman Street and the ancient Bernwode Forest from which it derives its name. Part of the woods are still there and muntjac or barking deer are to be seen, and in the wet oak and hazel woods, primroses and cowslips abound. From the 16th century, the village was a stopping place on the road between Warwickshire and London. 'Grendon Underwood, The dirtiest town that ever stood'. No doubt the state of the roads gave rise to this rhyme that has been handed down through generations.

Stories of rich tradition and legend come from John Aubrey, the antiquary, one of which is that Shakespeare passed through the woodlands of Bucks on his way to London from Stratford on Avon. There was a green track through Grendon, frequented by strolling players. It is believed that the bard used this path to arrive at The Ship Inn now Shakespeare House, where he would stay for the night. Tradition tells us that the characters, Dogberry and Verges were based on two Grendon constables who arrested Shakespeare for sleeping in the porch of the parish church. He was charged with robbing the church and when arrested, he asked that the chest be opened and finding nothing missing said 'much ado about nothing', which could have set the title for that play.

Shakespeare House is an ancient Elizabethan house near St Leonard's church. Oak framed with brick infilling, inside are large arched brick fireplaces with stone moulded facing. The gable has an oval window. It is said that this is the room in which the poet slept and composed.

When it was an inn, it could accommodate forty people. The

house has had a greater importance than the exterior. The Petty Sessions for the Ashenden Hundreds of Bucks were held there.

From papers found in an old iron chest at Doddershall, it is known that troops were mustered there. A muster notice, 1674, directs the 'Rt. Hon. Lord Lieutenant of the Countie commands souldiers appear at the signe of the Shipp in Grindon' on a certain date, 'compleatly armed and well fixed' and that they should receive 'Two dayes pay and each muskateere a pounde of pouder.'

A lady in the village remembers life here nearly sixty years ago. Then traders came to sell their wares, and a carrier would bring parcels and take away a bundle of rabbit skins. 'Calico Jack' came from Waddesden with haberdashery, another would bring greengrocery and take you to Bicester or Aylesbury in his pony and trap to catch a train, and a fishmonger called.

A 'Club Feast' was held annually in the village school. Women cooked a meal for which poor people had paid into a club. The first spring cabbage was always ceremoniously cut for this. A church service preceded the meal and a band played for entertainment. Peonies were fixed to the church flag pole to signify the event. This must have been a longed-for meal at a time when near starvation was not unknown in villages.

The tramway started in 1872 to serve the estate of the Duke of Buckingham. Later coaches were added for the benefit of adjoining villages. In the 1930s, students used it to reach Aylesbury grammar schools. They would cycle to a crossing between Grendon and Waddesden to board, but if they missed it, they had to pedal furiously to the next stop at Quainton. If the driver was good tempered he would wait, shouting encouragement, as they laboured along. The tramway ceased in 1935.

# Haddenham ❧

Church End Green is the focal point of the village. It was the Saxons who built a church by the side of the green, so maybe we owe this lovely scene to Hadda the Saxon thane. It is thought the name of the village came from 'Hadda's Hame' becoming Haddenham. The church as we know it today was built about 1215, at least it was begun then, the Lady Chapel being the oldest part. In 1295 Edward I granted Haddenham a Charter to hold a weekly market and annual fair. The weekly market has long since gone but we still celebrate our Haddenham Feast with an open-air service and a fair in late September every year. Once it was the high spot of the year when a day's holiday was given to all the farm workers (the only holiday other than Christmas Day) and sons and daughters from miles around came home for the fun.

The house names round the green tell some of their history; the Malt House where once there was a brewery; Eight Bells and the Anchorage which were both inns. Haddenham had a great many at one time. At the back of the pond is the entrance to Church End Farm which goes back in history nearly as long as the church and has a fine tithe barn. When the Norman Archbishop Landfranc held the church this was the seat of power for his agent.

Churchway is the main road through the village. Flint Street which leads away from the Church was once the main thoroughfare of the village. Its old houses are all picturesque and stand close to one another. In times past it was Duck Street, emphasising once the main trade of the village.

The Green Dragon is one of the most thriving pubs in the village. It's had an interesting past, as the manorial courts used to be held there. The Green Dragon was the emblem of the Earls of Pembroke who had authority here for a while after the Reformation. Someway further down on the other side is the Beehive, a village store (reputed to have a ghost). There has been a shop here for hundreds of years. It used to sell all kinds of things including items of clothing for the village families, but now it is a specialist grocer.

The old high walls in Haddenham are rather special. Modern ones are of breeze-block and rendered, but they copy the old, some still remaining, and they used to line every street. They were made of a kind of clay called witchert that is peculiar to this area. A stone base of about 18 inches was covered by the clay held in place until set by wooden shutters. Cottages used to be built like this too and the Baptist and Methodist Churches in Haddenham are built of witchert. The tops of the walls were thatched to keep the wet from going down into the clay. From this sprang the old saying 'Silly Haddenham who thatched the ponds to keep the ducks dry'. Not really so silly as the wide eaves over the pond sheltered the little ducks who do indeed drown if their early feathers are not protected from the rain.

# Hambleden 🌿

Hambleden Mill today stands sentinel on a backwater of the river Thames at the entrance to the beautiful Hambleden Valley, as it did when recorded in the Domesday Book. It remained a working mill until 1958 and, although recently converted into modern flats, the exterior appearance has been retained. The mill race still meanders by and now creates a marina. A long walkway over the weir leads to the lock and a short distance along the towpath towards Henley the imposing house 'Greenlands' comes into view. Once the site of a siege during the Civil War, it later became the setting for a Victorian mansion where the Rt. Hon. W. H. Smith, M.P., son of the founder of the bookstall business settled in 1858. It is now the Henley Management College.

The first landmark on the road to Hambleden is Yewden Manor with its ancient avenue of yew trees. A modern car park nearby serves the needs of visitors to the river and close to this is the site of a Roman Villa which was excavated in 1914.

The present Manor House, dating from 1604, is situated in the village itself. Lord Cardigan, leader of the charge of the Light Brigade, was born there. Since 1923, the manor has been owned by the W. H. Smith family, bearing the name of Viscount Hambleden.

The village buildings form a triangle around the village pump— still in full working order beneath its chestnut tree. The parish church stands commandingly along the northern edge. Its origins date back to ancient times, but much has been rebuilt, extended and restored over the centuries. Four weather vanes of local ironwork surmount the tower which houses six bells still regularly rung.

The houses of the village are a blend of brick, flint, wood and plaster, some part tiled, but form a harmonious entity. Great care is taken to maintain the attractiveness of this unspoilt village. Even the telephone box has been incorporated into the post office wall and the petrol pump housed within the garage building. The village amenities also include a general stores, smithy, butcher, builder, tree specialist and The Stag & Huntsman, as well as a Parish Hall, social club and the doctor's surgery. The village school was originally situated in what is now part of the Parish

Hall. The new school was built on the hillside overlooking the village in 1890 to commemorate Queen Victoria's Golden Jubilee. As long ago as 1820 there was a lace school where local girls learned also to read and write. Lacemaking and straw plaiting were local industries in the last century.

Although the village lies centrally in the Hambleden valley, it contains no farms. The farmhouses and buildings, both ancient and modern, are dotted around at Mill End, Rotten Row, Borough, Chisbridge, Rockwell End and Colstrope. Smaller farms have been absorbed into larger ones and a number have become private dwellings.

# Hanslope

Hanslope is situated in the north of the county bordering North-amptonshire on three sides. It is sandwiched between the M1 motorway and the main line railway from London to Scotland. The Grand Union Canal is just outside the parish.

The church is a noted landmark having one of the finest steeples in Bucks. Built in 1250 on a high ridge, it is said that seven surrounding counties can be seen from the battlements.

The beautiful octagonal spire of Ketton Stone is 186 feet high, although the original was some 205 feet. This was destroyed by lightning in 1804. The weathervane on top is a model of a whippet type dog with an arrow through its paw. It was given to the village by a member of the Watts family, formerly squires of the Manor, whose life was saved by such a dog while serving in India.

Buried in the churchyard is a prize fighter named Alexander McKay, a native of Glasgow who died in 1830 aged 26 years after fighting Simon Bryne in Salcey Forest. These fights were illegal and when McKay was knocked unconscious he was carried to the Watts Arms in the village where he later died. Bryne was arrested at Liverpool three days later when he boarded a boat bound for Ireland. He was tried for murder at Buckingham but was acquitted and died some years later after another fight.

Although the vicar objected, a stone was erected on his grave under cover of darkness bearing the following epitaph:-

Strong and athletic was my frame,
Far from my native home I came,
And bravely fought with Simon Bryne
Alas but never to return.
Stranger take warning from my fate
Lest you should rue your case too late
If you have ever fought before
Determine now to fight no more.

A member of the great clock-making family Joseph Knibbs came to live at Hanslope in the late 17th century. He began clock making in Oxford where he worked with his brother John for many years. He then started a business in London and later moved to Hanslope where he continued making clocks, some of which are to be seen in the British Museum.

On 21st July 1912 the squire of the parish Edward Hanslope Watts was shot by his gamekeeper William Farrow as he returned home from church with his wife. The gamekeeper then turned the gun on himself. The Watts family had the road diverted and to this day the entrance to Hanslope Park, now owned by the Foreign and Commonwealth Office and used as a communications centre, is set at an angle and the spot where the murder took place is fenced off.

Hanslope was the centre of the lace making industry in the 19th century. As many as 500 women and children were employed in this trade, working long hours often by candlelight in order to produce lace for the buyer who called weekly and paid them about 6 pence a yard.

Most of the men worked on the land until the coming of the railways when many found employment at Wolverton Works five miles away.

With the development of the new city of Milton Keynes the population of Hanslope has doubled in recent years and a survey shows that many residents travel long distances to their employment, some journeying the 50 miles to London daily.

# Hazlemere

Hazlemere, situated on the outskirts of High Wycombe could once have been called Hazlemoor as this name appears on old photographs on the wall of the post office.

Deadman Dane Bottom was the name given to a deep ravine in Hazlemere running at right angles to the high road from High Wycombe to Amersham and now known as Eastern Dene. It was part of a wild moorland called Wycombe Heath.

There were very few houses in Hazlemere before the First World War. The scientist, Sir William Ramsey lived at Beechcroft on the main road. He won the Nobel Prize for chemistry in 1904 and was the discoverer of Argon and other gases. Later Beechcroft's name was changed to Tylers Wood and became a Royal Grammar School boarding house.

The Misses Carter, two ladies from High Wycombe concerned about the children in the area, founded a school somewhere between 1835–1840. This is thought to have been a 'dame school' in a building near Giles farm, now part of a huge housing estate. A few years later in 1845, largely through their energy and determination, they had a church built in the area and dedicated to the Holy Trinity.

In 1847 Hazlemere Church School was built and for over 100

years was the only school in the district. Pupils came from far and near and some came through Kingswood from Totteridge bringing their sandwiches for midday. In the old log book 1900–1910 it is recorded that fees for pupils at the school went up from one penny to tuppence a week. Work was disrupted by parents who came to the school to protest that they could not afford the extra penny. The headmistress had to send for the vicar to reason with the parents.

Since the Second World War Hazlemere has grown very quickly. There are now big private housing estates, many shops and an 18 hole golf course in the area.

# Hedgerley ﹏

The name Hedgerley dates from the time when the southern slopes of the Chilterns were colonised by early Saxon settlers.

Hedgerley was famous for its bricks. The brickmaking industry here probably dates back to medieval times but it had its heyday in the 17th and 18th centuries when several writers extolled the merits of Hedgerley loam. Its popularity resulted from the fact that the loam contained a large amount of sand and so made very good firebricks. Hedgerley bricks were used to build the Box Tunnel in Wiltshire on the main Bristol line of the Great Western Railway. Isambard Kingdom Brunel was in charge of the operation. Before the end of the First World War, when the Slough Trading Estate was built, brickmaking was the only form of employment in the area, other than agriculture or market gardening. But sadly brickmaking in Hedgerley came to an end just before the Second World War.

Many famous names have been associated with the village including Judge Jeffreys, whose children's marriages are recorded in the church registers. Well known Quakers are also said to have met in the Old Quaker House in the mid 17th century, and suffered harassment from Judge Ambrose Bennet who, locally, was more infamous than Judge Jeffreys. Another man of note was John Hill, the son of Theophilus Hill, Rector of Hedgerley from 1743–1746. The *Shell Book of Firsts* notes John Hill as the first daily newspaper columnist. He was the first biologist to introduce Linnaeus' binominal system into English science, making him the

originator of many generic and specific names. He wrote the first
English book on honey, and pioneering works on geology and
gemstones. He was also the first man to express in writing the
connection between tobacco and cancer.

Hedgerley has no stately home within its boundaries, and the
only mansion (Hedgerley Park) was demolished in 1930. But it
does have many old houses and farms of interest, some of which
date back to the 16th century.

One house with a ghostly connection is Leith Grove, in Hedgerley Green, a hamlet next to the village of Hedgerley. It was built in
1580 to serve as gamekeeper's cottage on the old Hedgerley Park
estate. It was here that Leslie French lived. When he and his friend,
David Lloyd-Lowles, moved in (in 1931) they were told that in the
late 18th, or early 19th century two men came to the house and
killed the old lady who lived there in order to gain a body – body
snatching being rife in those days. Some time in the 1940s a child
was given the spare room, and in the morning she asked her

mother who the nice lady was who had come to tuck her up. It was, in fact, the old lady who had been murdered. She appeared quite often to children, including those of families who had previously occupied the house. They thought her quite pleasant but were puzzled because she never spoke. When there was an adolescent there, the spirit became a poltergeist.

The work pattern of the village has changed considerably over the years. In the Roman period Hedgerley really established itself as an important centre for the production of pottery. In medieval times brickmaking was the main industry, and this reached its peak in the 17th and 18th centuries. In the 18th century most of the residents were either in domestic service or tending the gardens and farms on the Bulstrode, Hedgerley Park and Hall Barn (Beaconsfield) estates. Others worked in the brick and tile works at various points along the valley.

The original village at the bottom of Hedgerley Hill has remained relatively unchanged, and has been declared a conservation area. But in the 1930s some private development was allowed at the top of the hill, and in the early 1950s a new council estate was built there, and this tended to change the pattern of village life. Most people travel outside the village to work – in London, at Heathrow Airport, in factories on the Slough Trading Estate, and in both National and Local Government.

But all in all present day Hedgerley is a very beautiful and friendly village in which to live.

# Hitcham

The hamlet of Hitcham lies between the villages of Taplow and Burnham. It is mentioned in the Domesday Book, at which time about thirteen families resided there. The ancient church of St Mary dates from about 1126 and in that century the first stone building was erected, of which the present nave walls appear to have formed a part.

The Lords of the Manor were often high-ranking officials of Church or State and the cottagers mainly would work for them, or for the tenant farmers. They lived near the manor house, which was north of the church. Lord Grenville – Prime Minister in 1806–07 – purchased the house in 1780 and the Lordship of the

Manor in 1796. He acquired more land and built a new house called Dropmore Lodge. The old manor house became a school but was destroyed by fire in 1840.

Lord Grenville and his wife both died in the middle of the 19th century. Mr George Hanbury then bought lands around the church, including the old manor house site. He built Hitcham House, which still stands to the south of the church. He built a school (two rooms costing £350) and a reading room.

New roads, a new bridge over the Thames at Maidenhead and the coming of the Great Western Railway caused New Town to spring up in the south of Hitcham parish. There were a few shops and a pub, the Retreat. The general store, kept by Mr Wakefield, offered haircutting among the groceries! The shops have now changed or vanished. Some of them, being wooden, literally fell down. The public house moved into larger premises and still continues today, as the Maypole Inn. This area became the new centre of population.

In the north of the parish stands Nashdom Abbey. The name Nashdom is the Russian equivalent of 'Our House'. This property was built for Prince Alexis Dolgorouki in 1907–8 who engaged Sir Edwin Lutyens as the architect. The prince and princess did not live long in their impressive new house. They were both dead by 1919 and are buried in the churchyard of St Mary's church. This grave has a monument which incorporates a Russian icon. After 1919 the house was leased for a time to various tenants and in 1924 became the property of a community of Anglican Benedictine monks. It is the only Abbey of Benedictine monks in the Church of England.

# Holmer Green

'People just don't want to move from Holmer Green' commented someone on the fact that many try to secure another house in the village when requiring a larger or smaller property. This thriving community of around 5,000 lies on the plateau of the Chilterns between the Misbourne valley to the north east and the Wye Valley to the south west, over 500 ft above sea level.

Although references to the Manor of Holmer may be traced in the Domesday Survey, by the middle of the 19th century Holmer

Green was still only a scattered formless settlement; but the appearance of the village was transformed almost overnight with the adoption of the Inclosure Award of 1854 involving as it did a new pattern of roads and fields and the ploughing up of large tracts of common land. One important feature of this new layout was the Holmer Green Common, allotted to the Lord of the Manor on condition that it was to be fenced in, stocked with sheep and used for the recreation of the inhabitants. When a hundred years later Lord Howe sold certain land in Holmer Green together with a corresponding part of his interest in the Lordship of the Manor, the purchaser very generously decided to give the Common to the Parish Council, in whose possession it now remains.

One feature of the Inclosure Award was the dedication of certain ponds or watering places to the public. One of these was Holmer Pond itself, which was elaborately improved by the Parish Council about twenty years ago and is now a most attractive feature and focal point of the village. The Pond Committee is responsible for keeping its surround well stocked with flowers and shrubs, not forgetting the ducks which tend to get overfed by enthusiastic children.

In the early part of this century timber conversion and the turning of chair-legs (by 'bodgers') were a staple occupation in cottage workshops or in the woods, while other labour was absorbed by the local chair factory in Factory Street (renamed Orchard Way). In June the village became a rather noisy place because of the various devices to scare the birds away from the cherry orchards! Tambour beadwork was carried on right up to the present day, and past examples have been known to embellish the gown of famous actresses and even a royal bride.

Today many Holmer Green residents commute to London or to its outskirts as well as working in High Wycombe or other nearby towns. Employment is also provided by the many small firms on the Chiltern Trading Estate in the village.

An outstanding feature of Holmer Green has been the rapid expansion of its population which more than trebled between 1946 and 1974, and this has been reflected in new housing, modern roads, pavements, street lighting and greatly increased traffic.

One casualty of this development is the house Polidores where the young Dante Gabriel and Christina Rossetti used to stay. This is commemorated by a small close called Rossetti Place. An interesting building still standing is Pear Tree Cottage, built in 1703. In the 18th century it was a place of refuge for travellers crossing Holmer Heath and known as Workhouse Cottages. This building now belongs to the Parish Council – a Council house with a difference!

No such short account of a village and its history can do justice to the people – from all walks of life, whether natives or new-comers – who through the years have helped to build up the lively, friendly and hard working community we know today. As some-one has remarked, in spite of all its development Holmer Green is still a village at heart.

# Horn Hill 🐝

Horn Hill was meant to have been a model village and, where the Hall now stands, there were at the turn of the century, six picturesque cottages but without 'mod-cons'. Mr H. D. Harben, the then Chairman of the Prudential, bought Newland Park and much of the adjoining land, farms, and above-mentioned six cottages. On inspecting his agent's book, he saw that one cottage was rented by someone and found it to be a young man who used it in the week-nights for a games and reading room for the youth of the locality and, on Sundays, for a Sunday School and evening service. He refused to take more rent and said that he would build a suitable building for the Sunday work and a recreation room. It meant the demolition of the cottages, and, firstly, he built 12 cottages in three blocks of four higher up in Roberts Lane, and as a temporary measure, let the young man have rent-free a cottage he owned up Rickmansworth Lane. He intended making a model village of the whole area, but alas he died in 1910 before comple-tion of the Hall. The Village Hall was being built on the site where had stood the six cottages opposite the small church – St Paul's – a Chapel of Ease.

Mr Eric Harben, his son, had the Hall completed and he opened it in 1911. Mr Harben was a barrister and he drew up the rules for the running of the Hall. Unfortunately, the First World War made it impossible for Mr Harben to carry on living at Newland Park, so that the model village his father had envisaged did not come to pass. So many people have wondered why such an outstanding building is found in such a rural setting, and one wonders what Horn Hill would have been like had Mr Henry Harben lived and had fulfilled his dream. The first 12 cottages were the beginning of the dream, and the Village Hall was and is a monument to his memory.

# Hughenden 🐝

Hughenden has become very well-known because Benjamin Disraeli, Earl of Beaconsfield, lived at Hughenden Manor from 1847 until his death in 1881. Queen Victoria sent primroses, his favourite flower, to his funeral and these were placed on his grave in Hughenden churchyard, which is visited annually by the Primrose League.

The name Hughenden is derived from Hughendene or Hitchenden signifying the dene or valley of the Hitchen. The Manor, not far from the Church, is now National Trust property and open to visitors most of the year. There are rooms exactly as they were in Disraeli's time and many mementoes of the great man.

St Michael and All Angels, 'The Church in the Park', must be situated in one of the prettiest sites in the country, with Hughenden Park on one side and farmland on the other. There has been a church there for over 800 years. Those with Second World War memories can recall the stained glass east window being shattered by a flying bomb and then delicately being put together again using most of the old glass. There is an unique memorial to Disraeli in the church from Queen Victoria reading 'This memorial is placed by his grateful Sovereign and Friend Victoria R.I. Kings love him that speaketh right. Proverbs XVI 13'.

The Church House in the south-west corner of the churchyard is a medieval building which housed a small community of monks. It was restored in 1930 by Coningsby Disraeli and contains a minstrels gallery.

Hughenden gradually developed from the church northwards with a farm, cottages and now estates on what used to be extensive orchards, mainly cherry. There are still some of the original old orchards left in gardens. A delightful stream meanders by the farm and under a pretty bridge, flowing and broadening into the Wye in

Wycombe. Springs were very prevalent in the valley, causing some flooding, but these have now subsided, helped by a modern pumping station, from which half a million gallons of water are pumped daily from a 200 ft well.

Further along from the farm along the busy highway the mainly residential area is reached, with pleasant houses and gardens. A good proportion of young people with families live here and also retired folk. Daily many commute to their place of business in London and nearby towns.

Hughenden valley is a beautiful place, and, as most people say – 'We wouldn't want to live anywhere else'.

# Hyde Heath 🐝

Hyde Heath, the name for which possibly comes from 'the heath belonging to one William de Hyde', is described in one guide book as, '. . . a common with small houses . . . probably an early squatting settlement' and in another as 'a scattered district on high ground'. Neither of which are accurate descriptions of our present-day village, to which three parishes can lay claim, their boundaries converging on the Common.

In the latter half of the 19th century, the Ordnance Survey map shows little evidence for the village of Hyde Heath. There were a small number of houses clustered around Brays Green, a similar number around an inn on what is now the Common and a more significant number at what is now Hyde End. The map marks Hyde Heath 1½ miles north west of the present village. At that time most of the people would have worked on the local farms and in the houses of the local gentry; the nearby Shardeloes Estate and Hyde Hall, where Disraeli stayed, (now Hyde House) being notable examples.

During this century a mixture of different types of houses have gradually been built to give the village its present form, spreading away from the Common to the south. These developments have given the village a new lease of life; children for the school, support for the many societies and customers for the village shops.

As there is very little employment in the village itself and being near the railway station at Amersham, many residents work in London. People also commute to the nearby towns of High

Wycombe, Aylesbury and Amersham. Despite working outside the village, however, residents old and new have developed a pride in their village and the beautiful surrounding countryside.

The Common has only been the open mowed space it is now for about 25 years. Previously it was covered in scrub and gorse and criss-crossed with paths to the cottages and the old chapel. Now there is a cricket pitch, pavilion and a children's play area. It is the scene each year of the village fete; primarily a fundraising event in aid of the Village Hall. The amount of talent drawn out by this type of event is amazing and most of the village lends a helping hand.

The village can boast of no ghost, scandal or legend but it has one claim to fame. In the last war, one enterprising lady applied to the Government for extra sugar to enable her to preserve fruit with her own canning equipment. The idea grew until the house, now demolished, was converted into a small but highly successful canning factory. It received its crowning glory with a visit by Queen Elizabeth (now the Queen Mother) in 1940.

Hyde Heath is a coming together of old and new, a village off the beaten track, in very few guide books and on the edge of most maps. A village most people would not give a second glance to; but for those of us who live here in the charm of the Chilterns, it is a village where it is almost impossible not to join in the enthusiastic life of the community. Long may it survive.

# Ibstone

The small village of Ibstone straddles a ridge of the Chiltern Hills approximately ten miles west of High Wycombe. Some village points afford magnificent views of the Hambleden Valley below. The origins of Ibstone go back before the Norman Conquest and the village was included in the Domesday Survey of 1086 at which time it was called Hibestanes.

Merton College, Oxford, has been associated with the village from 1270 until very recently when John Paul Getty Junior purchased their common land holdings. In 1284 there were 26 tenant farmers. Their holdings ranged in size from very small to 25 acres with over half being of 10 acres or more. Ibstone remained a farming community until mains water and electricity came into the village in 1935. In 1852 the first of the present school buildings was erected. At that date the village population was 310 with some 50 children at school. There were five farms, two pubs, a grocer, post office, a wheelwright and a blacksmith. The village was a thriving self-supporting community.

There has been a church for over 1,000 years. The present building dates from about 1200 and has many interesting features including one of the oldest wooden pulpits in England. Like many villages, Ibstone has a windmill – Copstone Mill which was originally built in 1274. The present building dates from the 18th century and is an unusual 12-sided smock mill. This mill has featured in many films and T.V. productions but will principally be remembered as the family home in *Chitty Chitty Bang Bang*.

John Wesley recorded that he preached at Ibstone on two separate occasions in 1767 and 1769. It was not until 1862 that a Methodist Chapel was established which continued to be used as a religious meeting place for approximately 100 years. Local legend has it that an attempt was made to build another church on a new site in Grays Lane, but the Devil objected to a church being built on his property so that the rising structure repeatedly fell giving that particular spot its present name of Hell Corner.

A village custom is carol singing. A group of singers led by the headmaster visit every house in the village on the two evenings before Christmas and receive hospitality from many homes.

The village has held a firework display and bonfire on the Common on November 5th since the early 1970s. Soup and sausages help to keep out the cold. One of the major events in Ibstone's calendar is the village show and fete which is organised by the local Horticultural Society and is held on the Common on the second Saturday in August. This is a very popular event which attracts many people from South Bucks. Any profit is donated to local charities.

# Ickford

Ickford is a small village surrounded by pasture grazing for cattle, sheep and horses.

The river Thame is the boundary between Oxfordshire and Buckinghamshire, and every August since the Queen's Coronation in 1953 there has been a tug of war between Tiddington in Oxfordshire and Ickford in Buckinghamshire, over the river. One team, if not both, end up in the river! People from both villages come to watch the pull and make it a fun evening.

We have two public houses, The Royal Oak, and The Rising Sun. They are well known in the village as good meeting places and both are old country landmarks.

We have a lovely Village Hall, built by the men and women of Ickford. Lots of hard work went into this hall and it is used by many village societies.

Ickford has a lovely old church, dedicated to St Nicholas. The date of the first church here is not known but it was probably of wooden structure built in Saxon times. The earliest part of the present church is the chancel, the centre aisle of the nave and lower part of the tower date from about 1170 to 1190. Ickford church escaped the wholesale restoration inflicted on so many medieval parish churches in the 19th century. In this case, poverty proved a blessing! Between 1902–1911, it was sensitively and carefully restored under the direction of Mr Oldrid Scott, who managed to preserve most of the genuine medieval features.

Gilbert Sheldon (1598 to 1677) was Rector of Ickford and later became Archbishop of Canterbury, from 1663 to 1677. He gave a lovely chalice and platter, which we have on show at Christ Church, Oxford, as we thought it better to let people see how lovely it is.

This is a happy and caring village with a mixture of new and old houses. We have young families and elderly folk all enjoying village life.

# Iver Heath 🦢

Iver is recorded in the Domesday Book (Yfer – the word meaning a steep slope) but the first mention of Iver Heath (Everheth) seems to be about 1365. It was a sparsely populated area criss-crossed with many tracks and footpaths. Dick Turpin is reputed to have roamed the Heath.

The people eked out a precarious living from agriculture, and life must have been very hard for them. There was once a Workhouse perhaps an indication of just how hard the times were.

Our church, St Margarets, was built about 1862, and is a very beautiful building that blends into the countryside and did a great deal towards uplifting the people of the area at that time.

Over the years more and more people have come to live in the area and modern roads and improved transport have all contributed towards its growth. The famous Pinewood Studios where all the James Bond films have been produced, and which boasts the biggest studio in the world is within our borders, also Black Park where outdoor filming often takes place. The latter is also the venue for the South Bucks Agricultural Show which takes place annually.

Iver Heath W.I. was founded in 1920 and has flourished and grown since that time playing an active role in the village. During the Second World War they made meat pies under the National Pie Scheme – these pies were sold for ½d. profit each.

Another wartime activity was canning fruit and vegetables – the Institute owned the canning machine which could be used by people for a small payment.

Our new Village Hall was completed in 1966 with a grant from Bucks County Council and voluntary donations of many sorts. One fund raising activity was selling bricks for 1/- each, and this raised hundreds of pounds – if you bought a brick your name was on it! The Hall was officially declared open by Lord and Lady Drumalbyn.

New motorways, a mixed blessing, have given us easy access to other parts of the country and the M25 has actually removed quite a lot of the heavy traffic which thundered past a lot of houses for many years, so progress is not always bad.

# Ivinghoe

Ivinghoe is a picturesque village with old houses clustered on two sides of the village Lawn. The size of the church and the existence of a Town Hall tell us that Ivinghoe was once a much bigger village. In fact, Ivinghoe used to have two or three markets per week to which the local farmers and straw plaiters came to sell their produce.

St Mary's church is a large cathedral-like building dating back to 1230 with a 15th century roof. An enormous thatch-hook is attached to the churchyard wall. This was used to drag thatch from burning houses to prevent the spread of fiire. Opposite the church is the 17th century King's Head Hotel. The imposing 18th century Old Brewery House, standing between the church and the Town Hall, serves as a Youth Hostel but was once part of the local brewery as its name denotes. The Old Town Hall was last restored in the Queen's Jubilee Year and houses the village library. The downstairs was once an open market. Ford End watermill is a fine survivor from the days when many mills were at work in the Chilterns. It is believed to date back to at least 1795 and was still in use until 1970. The waterwheel is of the overshot type and two separate sets of stones were used, for grinding wheat for flour, and for animal foods.

# Jordans 🌿

About a mile across the fields from Seer Green lies the village of Jordans which takes its name from 'Old Jordans', the farm where Quaker farmers lived in the 17th century.

Jordans village originated when some land became available in 1915–16. A small number of members of the Society of Friends (Quakers) saw an opportunity to establish a village and community where artisans and others could apply their skills for the benefit of the community. Jordans Village Industries was formed, but alas, was not a successful venture and went into voluntary liquidation in 1923.

The village was designed to surround a green; building began in 1919 and commemorative bricks were laid under the first house on February 15th of that year, and on the nearest Friday to that date, a great supper is held, attended by as many of the tenants as possible. Building continued until 1923, by which time cottages

were built round the Green and a number of single houses, all of which are rented on monthly tenancies. The management of the village estate is vested in a committee of 12 members – eight elected by shareholders, three from what is called Tenant Members Committee and one from the Society of Friends.

The Old Jordans farm house was bought by the Society of Friends and is now run as a Guest House and Conference Centre. In the grounds is the Mayflower Barn, reputed to be built of the timbers of the Mayflower which carried the Pilgrim Fathers to America. This barn is used in the summer for concerts and many other events.

On the road to Beaconsfield is the Friends Meeting House, built in 1688. In the graveyard, among many other early Quakers, lies the remains of William Penn, the founder of Pennsylvania.

In the inevitable progress brought about by time, the nature of the village has modified, though much of the old spirit remains, and during the course of the year, many visitors come to visit the historic Meeting House and enjoy the lovely countryside around.

# The Kimbles ✤

Cymbeline's Mount, high in the hills in Chequer's land, was the stronghold of the British King Cunabelin or Cymbeline, from whom Great and Little Kimble derive their names. A gold coin depicting him was found here. Relics indicate that there was a Romano British village, a Roman villa and a Neolithic hill camp in Kimble hills.

The Kimbles consist of three churches, two schools, three pubs, a railway station, a garage, a cricket club and a much used village hall.

St Nicholas's church, Great Kimble, was famed for the stand John Hampden took against paying Ship Tax money in 1637. Legend has it that he galloped up the hill and into the church to make his protest to his assembled tenants and neighbours.

All Saints, Little Kimble, has stood for 700 years on Britain's oldest highway, the Icknield Way. An unspoilt medieval church, its greatest treasure is a series of 14th century wall paintings, recently restored and considered by an expert, Mr Clive Rouse, as 'artistically the best in Bucks'.

As early as 1636 there was Baptist witness in Kimble with people meeting in their homes. The present church was built in 1933 and is well loved and attended.

On Remembrance Sunday Scottish pipers, traditionally dressed, pipe the procession from St Nicholas to the War Memorial at Little Kimble for the service for the dead of two world wars, and then return to The Bernard Arms for refreshment.

The Crown mainly serves the villagers of Little Kimble. Annually a Harvest Festival has been held there. After the thanksgiving service, accompanied by Ellesborough Silver Band, produce donated is auctioned, the proceeds going to charity. Morris dancers also entertain there.

The Swan and Brewer is a free house. The open space in front is used for many things – for bonfire night, for the Beagles to meet, and also for the Vale of Aylesbury Hunt to foregather. Sometimes as many as 100 horses and ponies meet.

Kimble Cricket Club was formed in 1907 some three years after a Ladies C.C. was started. Most players live locally. It has literally been a family club to the Adams, the Spitalls and the Woolcott families. Frank Woolcott was outstanding with over 32,000 runs and 200 wickets to his credit.

The Kimble Point to Point Races are well known. The Queen is patron and the Queen Mother has attended. At the Easter meeting the Trumpeters of the King's Troop lead the field to the start. This event is held on Mr C. M. Robarts' land.

The Berkeley Hunt was changed to The Vale of Aylesbury Hunt several years ago. The livery colour is old tawny, that of the Earl of Berkeley. They meet at The Swan and Brewer as do the Old Berkeley Beagles.

The inhabitants of Kimble include farmers and farm workers, engine drivers, Lloyds underwriters, caretakers, gardeners, architects, estate agents, motor mechanics, shop keepers and many retired people, among them nurses, postmen and journalists who all participate in village life.

To conclude, Kimble dwellers range from Baroness Berkeley who sat in the House of Lords for 18 years yet joined in village activities, to Freddie Foster who scythed the grass verges for innumerable ages and was known and liked by all.

A friendly couple of villages!

# Knotty Green 🌿

Adjacent to Forty Green and previously known as 'Naughty Green' this village lies along the main road between Beaconsfield and Penn in Chiltern District.

Just off the main road there is a charming cricket pitch with a small recreation area adjoining for the youngsters and, in one corner, an old dew pond now fenced off, which is known to have been used for sheep dipping and reputed to have been in existence for 400 years.

Opposite the cricket pitch stands Hutchins Barn – a 16th century timbered house with a minstrels gallery which, over the years has been modernised. Eghams Farm, built in Tudor times, is a private residence and stands on a path leading to Hogback Wood.

Baylins Farm retains much of its old character with flagstone floors and inglenook fireplaces, low ceilings and wooden beams.

Knotty Green is in Penn Parish and has many large houses standing in their own grounds with two large housing estates providing an overspill for Beaconsfield.

# Lane End 🌿

The village of Lane End (once called Ackhamsted) sits high in the Chilterns surrounded by acres of common land, hills and beech woods.

Two ponds, the Mill and the Foundry are both in the centre of the village and were used years ago in the Smith's chair factory and Hobbs' Iron factory. Much of the foundry work can still be seen around the village.

Before the Second World War Lane End was a very close-knit village, with many inter-marriages. Life was very hard for the very often large families living in the little terraced houses, many without mains water, electric light and only two rooms. Most homes had water tanks in their garden or could use one of the four wells around the village. Blackwell, which was filled in in the 1950s, has just been re-opened again.

The village then seemed to be self-sufficient. There were two bakers and the farms delivered the milk early in the morning straight from the can into the milk jug. The butchers slaughtered their own cattle, whilst Mr Goodchild the undertaker used to make the coffins in his little workshop near Botony Pond. There was even a muffin man with a tray of muffins on his head covered with a clean cloth!

The Clayton Arms Public House was built by the Claytons in the 17th century when they came to Lane End to escape the Plague in 1665.

Designated an area of outstanding beauty, Lane End attracts many walkers to its lovely Chiltern countryside.

# Latimer

Latimer is in the beautiful valley of the river Chess. The village is centred round a small triangular green, although the parish extends several miles in a mainly northerly direction.

The history of the village dates back to Roman times and there are the buried remains of a building thought to be about 80 AD.

The first mention of a mansion at Latimer is in 1194. In the 19th century it became the property of Charles Compton Cavendish who, in 1858 became Lord Chesham of Chesham.

In 1939 Latimer House was requisitioned by the government and used as an interrogation centre for German and Italian prisoners of war. At the end of hostilities and after the property had remained empty for nearly a year, a college for the joint services was founded. In 1983 this college was moved to Greenwich.

On the village green is the pump which supplied water to the residents until about 50 years ago, when the water company laid on a main supply; one tap per household.

Also on the green is an unusual obelisk in honour of local men who fought in the Boer War. By the side of this memorial is a stone mound bearing plaques with the following 'The horse ridden by General de Villebois Mareuil at the Battle of Boshof, S. Africa, 5th. April 1900 in which the General was killed and the horse wounded'. On the other side the inscription reads 'Villebois, Brought to England by Major General Lord Chesham KCB in 1900. Died 5th. Feb. 1911.' These features arouse great interest in the many visitors who admire the village of Latimer set in the most beautiful countryside of Buckinghamshire.

# Leckhampstead 🐌

The village of Leckhampstead is situated on the stream the Leck that rises in Whittlebury forest in Northamptonshire and is a tributary of the river Ouse which bounds the parish on the south side. In bygone years the parish was divided into two parts called Leckhampstead Magna and Leckhampstead Parva and land between was known as 'Tween Towns'.

It is possible to trace the owners of the manors or estates that comprised the village from the time of the Norman conquest. At that time Walter Giffard and the Bishop of Bayeaux were the principal landowners. In the reign of Richard I the Chastillon family held the chief manorial estate and the altar tomb in the north aisle of the church of a full length recumbent figure of a knight in armour is believed to be a member of the Chastillon family, possibly Hugh De Chastillon. By 1398 the estate had passed to the Gernons and from them to the Greenways and was then purchased by Edmund Pye, and through female descendants it was bequeathed to Martha Baroness Wentworth who before her death in 1745 nearly demolished the old mansion, but left the estate to a niece, Martha who married Lord Beauclerk. The manor is reputed to have a ghost which present-day villagers claim to have seen walking by the river. The ghost at Weatherhead farm carries a spinning wheel but both are reported to be quite harmless!

The church, dedicated in honour of the Assumption of the Blessed Virgin has its first rector recorded in 1219 and contains some rich remains of the Norman period.

Leckhampstead House was built in 1837 as a rectory by the Rev. Heneage Drummond, Rector from 1835–1883, and is now a private dwelling. During his incumbency the Rev. Drummond felt very strongly that the proximity of the local public house to both the church and the rectory was inappropriate – so he bought and closed the pub. Modern Leckhampstead has neither pub or shop and is now 'dry'.

Lacemaking used to be taught in a thatched cottage where Bellandean now stands, and Leckhampstead was one time well-known for its pillow lace.

# Ley Hill

In the past, Ley Hill was well-known for its gypsies and drunkards! The former for the good camping facilities and the profusion of hazel twigs (from which they made clothes pegs) on the Common, and the latter for the close proximity of the four Pubs – The Swan, The Crown, The Five Bells and The Hen and Chickens.

The population of the village has changed over the past 50 years from agricultural workers and brickmakers, to professional people. Bricks are still made locally but by machine, not by hand.

The Common, still a very popular recreational place, has altered in appearance since local farmers ceased grazing their sheep there in the late 1930s. This has resulted in the growth of many scrub oak trees, and the disappearance of the gorse and raspberry canes which used to grow in profusion.

Ley Hill is proud of its community spirit, and a quarterly Newsletter is published and distributed by the Village Hall Committee. A good variety of activities take place during the year, which cater for all sections of the residents. One of these events happens at Christmastime, and is much looked forward to, especially by the children. People assemble outside the Village Hall around a glowing brazier, and sing carols. Afterwards, mince pies and coffee are served in the Hall. Another traditional annual event is a Meet of the Old Berkeley Foxhunt on the Common.

# Lillingstone Lovell

Lillingstone Lovell is one of the most ancient and unspoilt villages in Buckinghamshire. At the time of the Domesday Book it was known as Lillingestane, and about 1431 it became the property of the Baronial family of Lovell, since when it has been called by their name.

Perhaps it was the plentiful supply of water from the brook and the spring that enabled the early farmers to settle here on the edge of the great Whittlewood Forest that covered the area in early times. To this day farming is the main livelihood of the local people.

The beautiful old village church, which has been the centre of the village life through the ages, is the third church to be built on

the present site. No trace remains of the original building. Of the second church built in 1210, the tower and porch arch remain and are incorporated in the present building. The monuments and hatchments within recall the history and generosity of the local notables.

In 1546 the Manor was given by the king to Sir Nicholas Wentworth and remained in the possession of this family until 1784.

The most famous member of this family was Sir Peter Wentworth, member of the House of Commons for Tamworth. He bore a conspicuous part in the attempt to resist Cromwell's encroachment upon the rights of Parliament. From the interest on money he left the parish, stem the Wentworth Charities.

The family lived in a mansion, built in the reign of Henry VIII, that stood behind the present Hall Farm. The last of the Wentworths bequeathed the estate to a relative. Shortly after his succession the Manor House was demolished, and the beautiful avenue of trees cut down. The foundations of the old house can still be seen in dry weather.

In 1836 the estate was bought by a member of the Delap family. Major James Bogle Delap and friends carried out an extensive restoration of the church in 1891.

The village has altered very little in appearance in the last 120 years. It is in a conservation area, and housing development is not permitted except for one or two dwellings built for agricultural workers.

The Church of England school was built in 1850, and the porch added in 1905. It remained as a school until 1916 when the children were moved to Lillingstone Dayrell school. An old log book, kept by the mistress, shows that the making of bobbin lace featured largely on the girls' curriculum. Lace making was a cottage industry for women, whilst the men worked on the land.

An event in 1923 changed the outlook and status of the village. The Manor and village farms came on the market when the estate was broken up. Some tenants bought their farms, and some people bought their houses. There was no longer a squire to rule the village and require the children to attend church and Sunday school — whether they would or no!

In a way this event brought a certain stability to the village. At the present time, some farms have been in the same family for three generations.

In the 1930s the village ghost appeared at the house of two old ladies up at Briary. People came from Northampton to see the lady on a white horse, but the ghost was exorcised once and for all when it was disclosed that the image was caused by trick photography!

# Little Brickhill 🐚

This village is mentioned in the Domesday Book. The Norman name of the village was Bryhulle, which in time became Brickhull, and eventually Brickhill. There is no connection in the name with the manufacture of making bricks. In medieval times the village was connected with the making of encaustic tiles. In the grounds of the present Grange ancient flues and ovens were discovered. The works are attributed to the 13th and 14th centuries and are monastic, being the work of the brethren of the great Abbey at Woburn.

The church, St Mary Magdalen, dates from the days of Henry II in 1154. The nave was completed in the 12th century and the tower was built in the 15th century. The Church Register begins in 1559, the 2nd year of the reign of Queen Elizabeth I.

In 1443 the village became the place for holding the Assizes which continued for nearly two centuries until 1638 – that is from the reign of Henry VI to that of Charles I. The traditional place where the Assize Court met is now Warren Farm. Although the conspirators of the Gunpowder Plot were not actually brought before the Brickhill Assizes, it was in this village on the 5th November, 1605, that Catesby and other conspirators were apprehended.

Prior to the coaching age there were five inns in this village – The Old Malting, King & Queen, Shoulder of Mutton (now White Maples), King's Head and the Bull. These inns, however, did not exist in the coaching era when in the half mile of Little Brickhill there were 14 inns at the same time. These inns did a roaring trade. Passengers from London to Manchester and Birmingham in both directions spent the night here and this of course meant an army of ostlers, stable boys, shoeing smiths, and for the coaches themselves, wheelwrights and coach repairers. One of the largest of the coaching inns was the George, which was only demolished some twenty years ago. It was on the site of the present George Farm. Today there exists only the Green Man and the George & Dragon.

The main A5 trunk road splits the village in half, making it very difficult for children to venture from one side of the village to the other unaccompanied. The A5 continues to be the biggest 'headache' of the village and after many years of fighting, at last the dream of the Ratepayers Association looks like becoming a reality as the by-pass has at last been agreed.

# Little Chalfont 🐿️

Our village is unusual in that it grew up as a result of the railway which came in the latter part of the 19th century. Before the railway arrived there was little except farms; Burtons, Nightingales and Cokes amongst others, all names of lanes now. Burtons farm is mentioned in the Domesday Book. The road running through the village, now the A404 was once the main road between Reading and Hatfield.

In 1904 the first shops were built and just opposite the original shops and station is 'Village Way', among the first dormitory dwellings.

Part of the growth of Little Chalfont has come from the Radio Chemical Centre, now Amersham International, which like Topsy has growed and growed culminating in a large office building opened in 1985.

The Rural Preservation Society works hard to preserve the more rural parts of the village and has done a wonderful job planting bulbs and ornamental trees, cutting the grass and making the centre of the village pleasant.

The M25 is a few minutes away and yet the lovely countryside of the Chess valley is less than five minutes away too.

# Little Hampden 🐿️

Nestling in the heart of the Chiltern Hills is the small community of Little Hampden. A hamlet of 24 dwellings, it is recorded in the Domesday Book.

A small farmhouse, smithy and cottage, are situated on what was a main road from London, and the forge is one of the oldest now working in the country. Re-built, following a fire, it was previously thatched, as is the 17th century cottage it adjoins, and was used as a staging post by the coaches on the 'London Run'.

Half a mile up the twisting lane, toward the main community, are two large houses built by the Atkinson brothers in the early 1920s. Courtfield House stands on the Cobblers Hill Road and Hampden Lodge, once known as Little Hampden House, was leased to the Women's Land Army during the Second World War, and when vacated by them, it was sold to the Earl of Buckinghamshire, who lived there until his death.

The diminutive church has had several additions over the centuries. Of Saxon origins, its walls have a unique collection of paintings, and clearly defined are St Christopher, and some of the seven deadly sins.

During the 1920s and 30s the village boasted a Village Hall, but this old ex-army hut was requisitioned for a bombed-out family from London in the early part of the Second World War. Since then the wooden structure has undergone a complete transformation.

The Rising Sun, probably erected about the same period as the farmhouse, recently underwent extensive alterations. The old brickwork was perfectly matched, though the interior bears little resemblance to that of even a short time past.

# Little Horwood 🐿

The village was known as Parva Herewode or Horwude in the 13th century, Parva Horwode in the 14th, Harwood Parva in the 17th, each name referring to the woods and the heavy clay soil in the area. When the field system was developed the Roman unit split into two parishes and Little Horwood became a village in its own right. It was not mentioned in the Domesday Book, being included in the Winslow manor which belonged to the Abbot of St Albans until the Dissolution of the Monasteries. Little Horwood's church, St Nicholas, was built about 1200 added to over the centuries and restored in 1889 when a series of wall paintings was discovered under a crust of whitewash. The earliest date from the 13th century.

The Second World War changed Little Horwood from a quiet rural community to one bustling with crowds of strangers for an airfield was made on land lying between the two Horwoods. It came into use on 3rd September 1942 and from it operated No 26 Operational Training Unit of Bomber Command flying mainly Vickers Armstrong Wellington twin-engined bombers, though many other types of aircraft came and went also. The constant din of aircraft flying low overhead became commonplace and crashes and the death of crews all too frequent. The army was camped at the Manor and prior to D Day, the village was seething with men and machines carrying out manoeuvres on a vast scale.

The airfield ceased operations on January 15th 1946 and a sudden quiet must have settled again on Little Horwood. To-day the runways and ammunition sheds can still be seen over the fields but the only activity is the grazing of sheep and cattle and the only flights are made by birds.

Life went quietly on; too quietly perhaps. In 1968 some felt that the village was lacking in amenities and much needed improving. There were black spots and very little in the way of entertainment. The village was losing its spirit.

So a newsletter was produced and put through every door. It was a gamble. Deficiencies were pointed out and a scheme was suggested to raise money for the suggested alterations and improvements. The letter ended thus:-

'Because of its smallness, the village must pull together or nothing can be achieved. It can only do this if everyone contributes in some way to the maintenance and running of the village, and the people of the community will only do this if their interest is aroused.'

The gamble was successful. The people rallied round. The Little Horwood Social Amenities Association was born and the Enter-tainments Committee came into being so that all that was wrong has been put right and within the village there is now an active social life.

One of the first achievements of the Social Amenities Association was to buy the school, closed and up for sale. This now houses a flourishing Play Group, the Youth Club, as well as being the Cricket Pavilion and a venue for dances, bazaars, parties etc. The cricket field and playground behind and surrounding it is in the charge of a committee who have recently enlarged and improved the facilities. Sports for the children and pig roasts and a barn dance are some of the activities which take place here. The village hall is used for similar functions, for meetings and for the annual theatrical production staged by the W.I. Shrove Tuesday Pancake races and May Day Celebrations have also been revived by the W.I. and in October there is the Village Race, a cross country event, open to all ages, 2½ miles for the younger men, 1½ miles for ladies, children and the not so young. The whole village turns out for this event either to run or just to watch. Several cups are presented and the Crown does a roaring trade. Boxing Day sees a race of a different kind when duck owners bring their birds, complete with knitted colours round their necks, to race in the brook. It is a crazy get-together which raises some money for the recreation ground. Racing of a more serious kind takes place in the spring when two point-to-point meetings are held on Manor Farm land if the weather is not too wet and the claysoil from which the village derives its name does not become waterlogged.

The money raising scheme first suggested in 1968 has continued to this day; weekly payments for those wishing to participate, a weekly draw to determine the winner of the week, and the profits managed by the Trust which allocates money to those organisations in need of it for improvements etc. Quarterly, the *Little Horwood News* is published, giving news of events, reports of functions, welcoming newcomers and frequently producing items of historical interest.

For the future, though people come and go, it is hoped that the community spirit which makes this village such a good one to live in, will continue.

# Little Kingshill 🦢

The origins of the village date back to around 900 AD when a monastery was founded where Ashwell Farm (Kingshall) now stands. William the Conqueror gave a Manor and lands to a Saxon nobleman, the Earl of Aufrics, but the lands reverted back to the Crown after the Earl's death. The road through the village was used by drovers of cattle being taken to market in London in medieval times and soldiers protected their progress and had barracks here. As well as Ashwell Farm there is a Tudor house, The Grange, next to the Common, Aufrics Farm of Elizabethan period, and Boot Farm dating back to 1660.

The coming of the Railway through Great Missenden at the end of the last century was a turning point, as people were able to go to business in London, and country houses began to be built for them. The village school too was built in 1887, and is still in use for pre-school children.

Life in the village was very different in the 1920s. No buses then, but there was a laundry, village store and bakery which included a sub post office, and the shops in Great Missenden delivered goods to the door. The baker came three times a week in a horse and cart, and a van brought fish, fruit and vegetables. Fresh roast and ground coffee and groceries from Mr Brown's shop and meat from Stevens the butcher were delivered weekly. The postman arrived at 7.50 a.m. precisely, on a bicycle and in uniform, to deliver letters posted the night before, and a second delivery in the afternoon at 4 p.m. At first there was no electricity, and grates and ranges did the heating and cooking, but soon it was connected and we stood by the switches and all switched on together.

The social life was vigorous and the old Memorial Hall was in constant use for many village activities.

Most men in the village then worked in High Wycombe in the furniture trade, and on the land, while the women did domestic work and bead and sequin work at home. This was sent down from London to one person who gave it out to the various workers and then collected and returned it. The traced material was stretched on a frame, wrong-side up, and the beads on long threads were hooked up from beneath.

The country around was famous for its cherry orchards and older residents will remember the guns banging off and wooden clappers clattering at dawn 'bird starving'. The Bucks black cherries are dark and small and perfectly delicious especially when cooked in cherry turnovers, the local speciality. Many people went cherry picking and casual labour was employed. Nearly all the orchards have been cut down to make room for the explosion of new houses built since the Second World War.

It is hard to tell what the people who live here now do for a living, as they leap into their cars and vanish for the day. Plenty of retired folk have come to enjoy the peace of the lovely countryside, though traffic, mowers, aeroplanes and screaming saws may have disillusioned them somewhat. Those newcomers who really take an interest are a splendid group and can be relied on to keep the village spirit alive still.

# Little Marlow 🦢

Little Marlow is a hamlet situated on the A4155, midway between Marlow and Bourne End, but its environs extend as far as Well End to the east and the by-pass to the west. Like many other areas along this stretch of the Thames it is steeped in history, being referred to in the Domesday Book.

The Manor House, built in the 16th century, stands in about 140 acres next to the church of St John the Baptist. These grounds were, in the 11th century, the property of Queen Edith. During the Second World War the Black Watch occupied the Manor House and Queen Elizabeth the Queen Mother and General Eisenhower inspected the troops and took the salute.

In the 12th century a small Benedictine Nunnery was founded along by the river near Spade Oak Ferry. One of the smallest monastic houses in England, it was suppressed in 1536.

According to people with roots in the village it was once a thriving area, with a jam factory at Westhorpe making jam with fruit grown in large orchards around the Pump Lane area. It is reputed there was once a saw mill in the village and many of the present older houses were originally shops – a bakery, confectioner, butcher, forge and coach house. The slaughter house being where 'The Saltings' is now and the Pound opposite where animals awaited slaughter.

As with all villages it has its scandals. There is one which is well documented. In 1919 Mr George Bailey, a milkman living in Old Barn Cottage, poisoned his pregnant wife. He sent his small daughter to relatives and tried to make his getaway. A neighbour, curious there was no movement next door, climbed to a bedroom window and saw Mrs Bailey dead on the bed. Mr Bailey was arrested on Reading station with several types of poison on him. He was tried at Aylesbury and duly hanged at Oxford. The case made history by having the first woman juror on a murder case.

There is also talk of ghosts. Many motorists involved in accidents claim they were trying to avoid a figure in the road, although they always disappear. At first they were thought to be excuses or drink, but one W.I. member clearly saw an auburn haired woman wearing a turquoise long sleeved nightdress in her bedroom, holding a cup. She stood facing the window and appeared lost and unreal. She then turned and disappeared through the closed door. Perhaps there is a lost soul roaming the village! Others have also seen 'something'.

There is some industry in the village. Wilton Farm, a thriving market garden of 364 acres is owned and run by the Emmett family. The sewerage works, which drains all the surrounding areas, is operated by Thames Water Authority and Folley Brothers operate a gravel and ready-mix concrete business, which covers about 140 acres. None of these are really large employers and most of the workers come from outside the village.

Most village activity centres around the recreation field and its pavilion. The field was left in perpetuity to the people of the village by Mrs Bradish-Ellames, as a memorial to those who fell in the First World War.

# Little Missenden

Those who now live in this small, close-knit village and pride themselves on belonging to a caring community, would have been horrified to have heard themselves described as a 'Godless lot', as were the villagers of the 1800s, when a well-known revivalist cleric of the time was appointed by Earl Howe, the patron, to the living. Objecting to the inadequate size of the vicarage, Earl Howe allowed him to enlarge and alter it, which resulted in a bill for £1,500, a lot of money in those days. When Earl Howe was presented with the bill, this was his answer 'I told you you could alter the place, I didn't say I would pay for it'. The repayment of this sum went on until the year before the Rev. W. H. Davis came in the 1920s.

The wonderful old church of St John the Baptist, over 1000 years old, owes much to the devoted love and service of its ministers. Within the memory of older members of the village is the Rev. ffolliott, who is remembered as the vicar with his pockets full of peppermints, and who used to dispense lengths of warm flannel to the poor of the parish. He was followed by the Rev. Fenn, and then Mr Davis, who is most remembered for the famous medieval wall paintings of St Christopher and St Katherine, which he was instrumental in discovering.

The village school, once a large establishment, serving the families in Hyde Heath and Holmer Green, is now a very sought-after First School. We are lucky that the school staff encourage their pupils, who mostly live out of the village, to join in our activities.

A different kind of school was the one where the Chiltern Hospital stands. This was originally Little Missenden Abbey. There is reputed to be a secret passage between the Great and Little Abbeys, used during Henry VIII's Dissolution of the Monas-

teries, but it has never been found. There is, however, a ghost at the Little Abbey. If you sleep in a certain room in the gatehouse on Twelfth Night, you will be aware of a presence, and experience the sensation of thumbscrews being painfully applied!

In the late 1930s, Little Missenden Abbey was a school for 'difficult' children, run on the lines of A. S. Neil's school in Sussex, with the emphasis on self expression and subsequently, it was hoped, self discipline. Boys from 7–11 years and girls from 12–19 boarded there, and it was run by Mrs Lister-Kay, a child psychologist and a friend of Eric Gill, whose studio at Speen was the venue for many young artists and musicians of the day. In fact for a while the composer Michael Tippett taught at the school, and Edmund Rubbra was a frequent visitor. Since the inauguration of the Little Missenden Festival of the Arts in 1960, the brain child of Mrs Pat Harrison, these two distinguished musicians have renewed their associations. Concerts featuring their compositions have been highlights of the event which takes place each October.

Few visitors to the village fail to gaze with admiration at the Manor House. Seen through the wrought-iron gates are beautiful lawns and gardens. This wonderful old part-Tudor building has been the home of many interesting people, notably Lady Alice Ashley and Brigadier Roger Peake, both of whom gave dedicated service to the Royal Family.

Finally, to complete the picture of our village life, we must mention the Village Hall. Once an old First World War army hut, this centre of our village activities, through the work and dedication of village stalwarts is now a very presentable renovated building, in continual use. Little Missenden feels it has a right to be called a 'caring and close knit community'.

# Long Crendon

Long Crendon was originally called Creodun, a Saxon word meaning Creoda's Hill, Creoda being the son of Cedric, or Cerdic, the first king of the West Saxons. A large village two miles north of Thame, it came into prominence towards the end of the 16th century with its needlemaking industry. Lacemaking likewise was one of its crafts, having been brought into Buckinghamshire villages by foreign refugees as early as the 16th century. It provided work for a large proportion of the women and girls, some of them learning even from the age of five.

Its long meandering main street, bounded at one end by the impressive 14th century grey limestone church, and at the other end by the Churchill Arms, is picturesque with its colour-washed houses and cottages, mostly of the 17th century.

Long Crendon's oldest inn, also in the main street, is the Eight Bells, situated towards the church end and close to the famous old Courthouse. These buildings fairly come alive each year in springtime when a group of dedicated people, old and young, come together in order to re-enact a selection from the York Cycle of Mystery plays in and around our lovely floodlit church. Then, for a memorable week, are you likely to come across all manner of colourfully-attired medieval characters as they emerge from alley and doorway! Ruth Pitter, poet and much-loved local celebrity, has been closely connected with these annual performances, now in their 16th year, and did indeed modify some of the original text.

Long Crendon, in common with many another village, seems to have had its fair share of ghosts! There was the poltergeist believed to have haunted the Courthouse, the galloping horseman of Lower End, an unhappy little lady in much the same area whose soul is now said to be shut up in a salt box buried in a chimney wall at The Mound, and the inevitable woman in grey who is said to haunt the church. She, like the rest of them, is 'friendly and harmless, and glides away to keep her secret'.

# Long Marston & Puttenham

These villages are pleasantly situated in peaceful countryside at the foot of the Chiltern Hills on the edge of the Vale of Aylesbury. The two villages, with their hamlets of Gubblecote and Astrope have a population of less than five hundred people. Most of these live in the village of Long Marston where there are about two hundred dwellings.

There are still twelve working farms in Long Marston and Puttenham but in the last twenty years land has been sold from several farms, the farm houses have become private houses and barns and cowsheds have been converted into expensive executive type dwellings.

Whereas a generation ago many local people were employed on the land with modern farming methods this is no longer the case.

There are several building and electrical firms in Long Marston. The largest local employer is the egg packing station at Gubblecote.

Many people commute to London from the railway station at Cheddington which is two miles away. Others work in the local towns of Tring, Aylesbury and Leighton Buzzard and at the cement works in the nearby village of Pitstone.

Visitors looking for the village pond in which Ruth Osborne, 'the last witch' was drowned, arrive only to find it is no longer in existence and the evidence of Long Marston's one claim to fame has gone.

# Longwick

On the borders of Bucks and Oxon, the village is as its name says a long village. It is seldom mentioned in guide books but is always on maps, having grown up over the centuries from a drovers road. Although primarily a farming area, new housing was built in the 1970s and there are new roads stating their ancestry: Sawmill Road, Wheelwright's Road and Barn Close.

One of the several listed buildings is Longwick Mill which whilst dating back to the 17th century is still run as a family business. Although this is now thoroughly mechanised the traditional buildings and old millstones are still to be seen.

The 1st of May is special in the minds of the children as they prepare garlands and sceptres of flowers for the parade in the playing field. Alison Uttley dedicated her book *Grey Rabbit's May Day* to the children of Longwick School. The custom is known to have been practised in 1850 when the children used to go from door to door chanting

'Good morning ladies and gentlemen
We wish you a happy May,
We come to show you our garlands
Because it is May Day
We only come here but once a year
So please remember our garlands'

The hamlet of Ilmer which completes the parish of Longwick-cum-Ilmer is home for about 70 people. Mentioned in the Domesday Book it is a very pretty place with village pond and it was at one time a town until like other places in the area its population was wiped out by the Black Death in 1349. It is now very much a leafy glade area and there are two horticultural businesses selling plants and Christmas Trees. The oldest farm house has a moat, not round the house, but round an island so that cattle kept there could be surrounded with water.

Owlswick is a friendly hamlet of 15 houses. The oldest dates from 1530. The Vale of Aylesbury Hunt meets at the Shoulder of Mutton each Christmas and there is an annual Easter Bonnet competition held there on Easter Sunday.

# Loosley Row & Lacey Green

Loosley Row and Lacey Green are really one fair-sized village in the Chilterns, an area of outstanding natural beauty, between High Wycombe and Princes Risborough. Lacey Green is on the ridge, Loosley Row half way up the side of the valley. They began as small farming settlements in ancient times but have expanded considerably. While the greater part of the land in the area is farmed, only a small number of people work in that industry. Some work in nearby towns or in other organisations in the countryside, such as timber research or R.A.F. Strike Command in the next village, others travel much farther afield, including London.

There is no stately home or old manor house warranting mention in guidebooks but Lacey Green does have some claim to minor fame, even notoriety in one case. One old house is Malmsmead in Kiln Lane where, in 1913, there lived Smithson and Sikes, expert burglars and housebreakers. These appeared to be respectable gentlemen, regularly travelling up to London by train to work, when they were in reality travelling to seventeen counties, from where the proceeds of their robberies were brought to the house in Lacey Green, which the police eventually raided. They eventually spent many years in gaol for crimes involving property to the value of a quarter of a million pounds, a fantastic amount in those days.

An outstanding feature is the smock mill which stands back from the road at the highest point. It is probably the oldest surviving smock mill and third oldest windmill in the U.K. and was built at Chesham in 1650, moved to its present site in 1821 and worked last in 1917. Chiltern Society members have worked voluntarily for years to restore it, with help from local firms and Wycombe College and it will be working eventually. The machinery, thought to be original, has been restored and a granary from Princes Risborough Town Farm has been re-erected next to the mill. It is open to the public on Sunday and Bank Holiday afternoons, with wardens from the Chiltern Society on hand to explain its restoration and workings.

Just down the road from the Village Hall is Stocken Farm, the largest farm hereabouts and much known and visited by the general public. Its known history goes back to the days of Elizabeth I, and the wife of the present owner has researched and made known many interesting facts about it. The farmer invites local school children to look over and learn about the farm and holds occasional open days, when many people go to what amounts to a 'fete' with educational entertainment, stalls and rides. Here the local entertainment society 'Lacey Green Productions' stage their bi-annual musical show in a large barn which normally stores grain, building a full-sized stage with theatre lighting and sound, scenery etc. The cast rehearses for weeks beforehand, the technicians working for much of that time; the calf-rearing sheds are used for changing rooms, loo tents appear, a field is made available for a car park for each night of the performances and the profit goes to a hospice for dying children.

Another place to visit is the Forge in Loosley Row, a craft industry which has been there for two hundred years, connected with the same family. Near, but just beyond the village, there is the Home of Rest for Horses, Westcroft Stables, Speen and the Pink & Lily public house, with its connections with Rupert Brooke the poet.

# Loughton 🦢

Change, rapid and irrevocable, is the potent force at work in Loughton now. Change, wrought by Milton Keynes new city. Change, starkly symbolized as never before by contrast between old and new: between the soft, golden, resolute tower of All Saints Church standing tall on its knoll overlooking Loughton Valley, and the intrusive, uncompromising, right-angled, mirror-spangled architecture, of Milton Keynes' new railway station a little way off. Doubtless the lovely 13th century church and the valley which has echoed to the footfall of prehistoric man and the march of invading tribes from Europe will have witnessed many changes throughout its long history. But the rapidity and finality of the present onslaught is a change in itself and can never have been equalled.

Memories persist, however, gifts from the past to reassure us of continuity. Customs, events, tall tales of notable characters and old ways of life, handed down the generations, some even immortalised in local features. Pitcher Lane, for example, with a well still extant; the water now used to irrigate local allotments. Along this ancient lane the denizens trooped to draw their water. A drudgery at the best of times, but sheer hell in winter, some small compensation perhaps drawn from a bath afterwards, before an open fire. The lane has changed, of course, many ancient dwellings have been demolished. But the emotive name lives on and one of Loughton's handsomest old houses, Becket House, the Old Rectory still stands there. Now a private dwelling, it was built in 1868 to replace an earlier rectory and in its turn has been replaced by a modern house. Surviving too, in quaint irony are some two-up — two-down cottages of meaner stamp, built for labourers, but which are now considered bargains at around £40,000 by city buyers seeking a better way of life.

Some older buildings of the village have been lovingly restored and converted. The old school makes a good example. Saved from demolition, it has been converted into a most attractive dwelling, and stands a monument to its owner's inspiration, and the determination of the village to educate its young.

Records of this determination reach back to 1848, before the school was built. Two rooms of Elm House, a Georgian Mansion, were allotted to this purpose. The records give us some essence of village life in Victorian and Edwardian times. Records of absences for legitimate reasons: infectious diseases, flood or snow-blocked roads, contrast with: bean-sticking, stone-picking, gleaning and the inability to pay the two penny weekly fee. There were also half-day holidays for religious and traditional festivals.

Of notable characters Charlotte Gregory must be worthy of mention. A skilled Victorian lacemaker, Charlotte worked well into her nineties. Her claim to fame, however, lay in her habit of clay-pipe smoking and her ability to expectorate her consequent pulmonary congestion with unerring accuracy from workspace to fire. It is said folk walked miles to marvel at the spectacle.

From Victorian times technological progress began to bite, accelerating through Edwardian years to radically alter rural activity. Jack Dolling, now retired, left a childhood baptised by the Brad'l Brook to enter a manhood of hard graft on the farm among beloved horses. His reaction to the first tractor in 1924 is unprintable! There are still horses in the village, however, at a thriving equestrian centre, catering for leisure and pleasure.

Jack also remembers the first bus. Here we can reflect on changing attitudes, for these early travellers thought nothing of alighting to enable the bus to negotiate the steep rise to the canal bridge at New Bradwell, and weekend revellers would disembark at a 'chippy' on the outward foray, to place orders for collection on the return. Try that on a modern city bus and see how far you get.

Loughton's oldest resident, Ethel Rose Foxely, remembers vividly the drudgery of the labour of her youth, matched by the uniformity of dress and pattern of life of the poor. The women wore black dresses with white aprons and worked afield, made lace, or walked to Bletchley to launder, for a pittance. A hard rural existence underpinned by well-stocked gardens and allotments, and a 'pig in the cot' to supply the table. The staple diet was the 'Buckinghamshire Clanger', boiled in a pot with the vegetables. This life has gone forever now, and perhaps we should be glad, but cold fingers of nostalgia will inevitably creep around the hearts of sensitive observers contemplating fields where foxes once barked and pheasants scurried, falling inexorably beneath the advance of the neat brick boxes, being marshalled along the new estate road that straddles the link with the old A5. At the sight too of the two old 'spit and sawdust' pubs on that ancient highway mercilessly shot up-market and where the ploughman no longer calls when wending his weary way homeward.

But in spring the high banks of Pitcher Lane will still bustle and bob with flowers, and yet offer a modicum of shelter from the blast of winter. Although the population is about to explode, the heart of the village will still beat for those who want to hear. There will still be some continuity for those who wish to feel it.

# Maids Moreton

In the beginning of the reign of King Edward I, the family of Peyvre or Peover, of Toddington (Beds), held a considerable estate in the area and two pious maidens of this family are traditionally stated to have founded the church, thus giving the village its name. Foxcote, the adjoining village had a minute church, now converted to a private dwelling, and is well known because the late Dorian Williams owned the manor house.

Mummers used to come round the village on Boxing Day. The players dressed as clowns and wore odd garments. They carried a black iron frying pan, a club etc. and sang:

> 'Here come I old Bel Ze Bub,
> In my hand I carry a club,
> Over my shoulder a dripping pan,
> Don't you think I'm a jolly old man?'

112

This was in 1926 when they were given a few coppers to buy beer. May Day was taken very seriously. Days before, mothers planned what sort of garland they would make for their daughters. Baby chairs, hoops, and crosses were prepared by binding mosses onto a base with twine and kept moistened with water. The evening before, they were decorated with the season's flowers – crown imperials (crown of pearls) were much sought after and were the high point of these artistic creations. Almost every child in the village went May garlanding.

Up to the beginning of the Second World War a baker in Main Street fired his oven (with faggots of wood) every Sunday morning. People brought their family joint of meat which was put on a rack over a roasting tin into which had been poured the batter for the Yorkshire pudding. Sometimes a fruit pie would also be taken later in the morning usually by the husband who would collect the whole meal on his way back from the pub later and taken home where the cooked vegetables were waiting.

There have been several 'characters' in Maids Moreton. One was Madam Morney, a member by marriage of the French per-fumers. She bought the Old Manor House opposite the Bucking-ham Arms in the 1930s. She gave a lot of work to builders in Buckingham and men who were unemployed in the village. She had a herd of Jersey cows and sold the cream at 6d for about 4½ ozs. A Q.C. Stewart Bevan lived with her causing great speculation amongst villagers – she being French!

Another character was Dick Jones, alias Captain Starlight who on returning from the First World War, had to leave his mother's terraced cottage in Batchelors Row when she died. He dug a pit in a field near Chackmore Farm, thatched it with straw, dug steps in the earth at the entrance, and lived there on bags of straw until his death. As his nickname suggests he was very knowledgeable about the stars.

In the 1930s there was much poverty, although folk were too proud to let it be known. When the blackberries and mushrooms were ready, the women rose early, got the children off to school, quickly did their housework and went off to gather blackberries and fungi. 'Blackberry Jack' always appeared with the same intentions and was very abusive if the women went near where he was gathering. Mr Busby, a greengrocer, came by trap from Buckingham each day and bought the berries (to make dye or jam) and the mushrooms for a few coppers per pound.

# Marlow Bottom 🦡

In the late 1920s it would have taken someone with a flair for predicting the future to guess that Marlow Bottom, which was then little more than rough fields with a muddy track running down the centre, would 40 years later provide homes for nearly 5,000 people. It was in the mid-1940s that the move towards development started. Families from the poorer parts of London who were experiencing nightly bombing found that they could escape for short weekends just for the down payment of £20 for a 40 ft frontage on the unmade-up road. These settlers, all do-it-yourself fans, had fiercely held views on what their new homes should look like. At weekends the valley hummed with activity, and at that time there were no disapproving planning officers looking over their shoulders to curb their eccentricities.

The first amenity for the new dwellers was milk delivered down the valley in a trap carrying the milk churns. Today what started so simply has become recognised as a highly desirable residential area, with developers hovering to pounce on the smallest plot of vacant land. However, traces of its country past can be found in the naming of 'Badger's Way', 'Oliver's Paddock' – Oliver being a much respected donkey – and 'Patches Field' where Patch the pony surrendered his rights to a much admired sheltered housing development. Also it is still possible to find some of the original downland flowers, including the Pyramid orchid and the Chiltern gentian.

A long established feature has been the Village Hall. This started inauspiciously as the 'Witches' Barn', a cafe that did not prosper. It had as neighbour a Nissen hut which was used as a canteen by Land Army Girls. This later became the Barn Club. Both these buildings have been modernised and are run by the Village Hall Trust. The most important annual event in Marlow Bottom has been the Rose Carnival and it was through the organisers that money was raised and targeted to buy and help maintain the playing fields. These are ideally situated and much used by local children.

The first President of the Village Hall was a Mr Folker, a flamboyant character who strode the valley in a large black sombrero and a black cloak. He had the good fortune to add to his life style by living in Dingley Dell. A partner to his eccentricity was a slightly demented lady who was to be seen walking in the valley at nightfall, wringing her hands, clothed only in her nightgown.

More recently Marlow Bottom has been able to celebrate having its own local hero. Stephen Redgrave brought back a Gold Medal from the Los Angeles Olympics, 1984 a record 3 Gold Medals at the Commonwealth Games in Edinburgh in 1986 and a gold medal from the 1986 World Championships for rowing. It seemed quite right that he should ride down the Bottom on the top of a double decker bus to universal applause. Another local resident, Margaret Beer, is well known for her hobby of restoring injured birds and animals to health.

# Marsh Gibbon

Most of the farms and stone terraced cottages are owned by the Ewelme Charity Trust, and the rents help provide for 13 poor men and two chaplains at Ewelme in Oxfordshire.

The Greyhound Friendly Society was formed in 1777 as a sick club. Today it has about 160 members and a 'Feast' is organised at the Village Hall following the parade to church with the Marsh Gibbon Silver Band leading the procession. The band celebrated its 80th anniversary in 1986.

The Parish Church of St Mary's dates from Norman times and the lovely old manor house stands nearby. Westbury Manor is situated near a moat in the centre of the village and Oliver Cromwell is said to have stayed at Cromwell House on his way to the Battle of Edge Hill.

The village has changed over recent years with small developments taking place. The new inhabitants have fitted into the way of life extremely well, many commuting to Oxford, London, Banbury, Thame, Aylesbury and Milton Keynes from here. In 1971–72 and 73 the villagers organised three successful steam rallies which helped raise enough money to build a new Village Hall which was opened in 1976.

# Marsworth 🌿

The Grand Union Canal runs through Marsworth with an arm of the canal going off to Aylesbury. The village is surrounded by farming country and was part of Lord Rosebery's estate. In the 1800s it had its own hospital but this was demolished in 1894 and the land is now known as Hospital Farm.

An elderly resident remembers trains on a branch of the railway line to Aylesbury, stopping at Marston Gate, just outside the village to pick up milk brought in from the surrounding farms for the Nestles milk factory at Aylesbury.

The canal was very busy at the beginning of this century. Boats carried everything but mostly coal, sand and wheat. In 1916 it was frozen over for six weeks and there was no movement of traffic at all with boats frozen in by the ice.

In the Second World War Marsworth became part of an airfield. The R.A.F. were there at the beginning of the war, flying Wellington bombers. They were followed by 4,000 American airmen who flew Fortresses and Liberators. A leaflet squadron was based there. The camp was a big one with a hospital, dining hall seating over a 1000, and a theatre. The stage from the theatre was later put in the village hall.

There was also an underground command post on the airfield. It was reported to be as big as a good sized bungalow and to be bomb-proof. It was kept well stocked with food and water at all times. Churchill was a regular visitor particularly towards the end of the war. He used to land there on his way to Chequers. General Patten also visited Marsworth and decorated some of the American airmen during a service held at the camp.

Although Marsworth has grown since those war-time years it is still a very happy and friendly place to live.

# Medmenham 🌿

The picturesque village of Medmenham nestles in the lee of Wooded Hill to the north and is principally a street of brick and flint cottages which straggles from the now discontinued ferry on the river Thames to its junction with the main Henley-Marlow road half a mile away.

The cottages and houses were built for the servants of the nearby large houses and estates such as Medmenham Abbey, Danesfield, Wittington, Kingswood and Harleyford Manor. In the past fifty years many of these large houses have taken on new roles. Some have been sub-divided into smaller houses or apartments, while others have become offices. In the village the cottages have been modernised, sometimes two combined to make larger properties and few modern houses erected. Fortunately no new estates have marred the beauty of the area.

The employment pattern has changed too and most of the residents now work far from their homes. The village itself has escaped serious industrial development, only the Water Research Centre has intruded upon the scene and it is screened from the river and village by trees.

At the junction of Ferry Lane and the main road is the ancient parish church of St Peter and St Paul, the road here is very narrow, and opposite is the cosy 14th century inn, the Dog and Badger.

Danesfield House, an imposing residence built in 1900 on a cliff overlooking the river Thames, was occupied by the Royal Air Force until 1977, when a Ministry of Defence Police Training Unit took over the buildings in the grounds and Carnation Milk bought

117

the house. The original Danesfield House was built in 1750 on a site previously occupied by Medlicotts, during the Middle Ages. A tradition had grown up locally associating the prehistoric earthworks in the grounds with the Danes who were known to have penetrated the Thames valley as far as Reading, some 15 miles further up-stream. In 1896 the Medmenham Abbey Estate was acquired by Mr Robert Hudson, reputed to have made his fortune with 'Hudson's soap'.

At the foot of Ferry Lane stands Medmenham Abbey, founded as St Mary's Abbey by the Cistercian Order in the 13th century. It later became derelict. However, in the 18th century Sir Francis Dashwood restored the Abbey and it is said to have been used by his 'Hell Fire Club' for orgiastic rites. It is now a fine residence overlooking a pretty reach of the river.

# Mentmore ✑

Rebuilt by Baron de Rothschild on completion of Mentmore Towers in the latter half of the 19th century, Mentmore is a pretty village with its mock Tudor houses set on top of a hill. The large village green is surrounded by splendid lime trees, and the views in all directions are quite breathtaking.

The church built in the 13th century is set on the highest point in the village with its 15th century tower as a landmark for miles around. It has over the centuries been added to and altered by various builders.

The dominant feature of the village was Mentmore Towers. Baron de Rothschild commissioned George Stokes to design the house, and the building was supervised by Stokes' father Joseph Paxton, who also designed the Crystal Palace. Work began in 1852, and on its completion Mayer Amschel Rothschild had the village of Mentmore rebuilt nearer to the gates of the Towers. No excuse for being late for work then! He also had stables and kennels for the stag hounds built.

Nearly everyone who lived in the village and the nearby villages of Crafton and Ledburn were employed in some capacity on the estate, in the studs, or gardens, the house, or management of the estate. There were very large gardens, with many greenhouses, and hothouses, for the estate was fully self supporting. When the last head gardener arrived, there were 44 full time gardeners. There were at least 10 laundry maids and dairy maids. The dairy was situated on the bend at the bottom of Stag Hill. It is now used as a smallholding.

The unmarried men lived in the Bothy, and there was similar accommodation for the grooms and trainers at Ledburn. Today this is the Hare and Hounds Inn.

One of the most interesting features of Mentmore were the Studs, for many famous racehorses were bred there, including winners of the Derby and the St Leger.

On the death of Baron de Rothschild the estate was inherited by his daughter Hannah. In 1878 she married the fifth Earl of Rosebery who later became Prime Minister. The Roseberys were a very sporting family and continued breeding racehorses right through to the present Earl's father.

When Lord Rosebery died in 1974, Mentmore Towers was offered to the Government of the day for 3 million pounds lock stock and barrel. There was quite a furore when it was turned down. The auction of the house and contents conducted by Sothebys caused much excitement. People came from all over the world to view and buy. The final sum realized was 6 million pounds, unfortunately many of the treasures were taken out of the country.

The Towers was finally sold to, and used as a conference centre for the followers of the Transcendantal Meditation Cult, and in the village as the houses become vacant they are sold off privately. The end of one Era and perhaps the beginning of another.

# Middle Claydon

Our village has no actual centre as such, but covers a large area, with a population of approximately 150. At one extremity we have Verney Junction, a handful of cottages which once housed railway employees, and a public house. The railway was axed by Beeching in 1967. There is one large house, probably an ex-farmhouse.

Claydon House has been home of the Verney family from the 17th century. It is now a National Trust property, although the Verney family occupy the South Wing. The cobbled courtyard probably looks similar to the days when dairying, laundry and carpentry were carried out. Views from the house over gardens, lawns and fields lead the eye to the three lakes, which years ago supplied the household with fish. Fishing is now confined to clubs, but a great variety of birds breed and dwell among the little islands.

Beside Claydon House stands All Saints church, with its 15th century tower, and painted ceiling in the chancel. High on the East Wall is the Gauntlet of Sir Edmund Verney, King's Standard Bearer, who was killed at the Battle of Edge Hill – his body was never found, only his hand, still clutching the Standard.

# Monks Risborough 🐚

The village of Monks Risborough derives its name from the scrub or 'hris', which once covered the hills, and the prefix from the Monks of Dorchester on Thames to whom the land was given in 993 AD by the Archbishop of Canterbury, in repayment of a loan.

Ninety years previously this estate, then known as East Risborough, had its boundaries outlined in a Saxon Charter. Many of these boundary hedges exist today, notably the Black Hedge which stretches from Waldridge, in the valley, to a point on the Lower Icknield Way. Recently it has been studied by a group of naturalists, who conclude that it had already been growing for 200 years before it was mentioned in the charter of 903 AD.

The old village is built in a rough rectangle at the foot of the Chilterns. Some of the cottages date from the 16th century, and to the joy of artists and photographers, many are still thatched. Among them is the old saddler's house where skins were tanned for working. The straight walk down the garden was used for stretching and twisting ropes, and the present owner still remembers, in her youth, helping with the stuffing of pillows for traditional lace making.

A pathway alongside one of the cottages leads to the 12th century church, dedicated to St Dunstan. Above the outer door of the porch is portrayed a pair of blacksmith's tongs converging on a face roughly carved in wood, illustrating how St Dunstan was reputed to have overcome the devil. This story is also reflected in a lead and fibreglass sculpture, complete with genuine Irish tinker-tongs, on the south aisle wall, made by a local sculptor in 1971.

Beyond the church, in a field which is now a children's playing field, there is a square stone dovecot, whose existence gave rise to the popular legend that an Abbey once stood here, but no evidence has been found to substantiate this.

In the Domesday Book there is a record of a watermill at Monks Risborough; and now, though the water-wheel has long since disappeared and the millponds are filled, a millhouse still exists on the site where the original mill must once have stood.

The parish boundaries enclose four other villages; Whiteleaf, Askett, Meadle and Cadsden.

Whiteleaf, or Whitecliff, contains several Tudor cottages and straggles along a metalled stretch of the Upper Icknield Way. Its name derives from the cliff-like appearance of the large cross cut in the chalk face of the escarpment. The first mention of this cross seems to have been made in the early 19th century in one of the Enclosure Acts, when it was referred to as 'This Ancient Landmark'.

Near the village centre is the Whitecross hall which forms a link between all five villages. It was erected in 1924 by the Monks Risborough W.I. on land given to them by a local property owner.

Cherry pie feast is an annual celebration at the Plough Inn in Lower Cadsden. It was first established to commemorate the death of John Hampden, who lived not far away, and died of his wounds at Thame in 1643, during the Civil War.

For the rest; the villagers entertain themselves, or are entertained at a variety of fetes, rummage sales, classes, bazaars and socials; or simply by walking over the valley and hills along the beautiful footpaths, with which Monks Risborough is so bountifully provided.

Meadle is now a hamlet home mainly to commuters who want to enjoy the countryside. There are several old cottages, some thatched by a local man, in an area which was a thriving farming community. Aylesbury ducks were bred for sale in the London markets.

Long ago Meadle was associated with the Quakers when a Friends Meeting Place was established in the 15th century known as the House of John White.

# Naphill 🎐

According to records, at one time Naphill was just a clearing in the woods, a bolt hole for petty criminals, and the Common was a stop on the drovers' route from the west. Today, approached by a very steep winding hill from Hughenden Valley, it consists of a long main road high on a ridge which, until the 1940s, was bordered by hedgerows, orchards, fields and a few cottages and houses. Since Bomber Command (now Strike Command) settled at the north western end of the village, bringing an increase of traffic and houses, these natural boundaries have been replaced by pavements, brick walls and constant house building. But on either side footpaths abound, leading to a wealth of scenery – meadows, cornfields and beechwoods carpeted with bluebells in spring and in autumn a riot of colour.

In the 19th century there were plenty of industries – stone cutting; chalk mining (which in recent years has resulted in subsidence); brick-making from Naphill's clay cap; Baldwins, an engineering firm to which Wycombe chairmakers would walk on Saturdays to buy small hand tools; blacksmiths; wheelwrights . . . all now gone. The late Jack Goodchild was one of the last remaining chair bodgers, a skilled craftsman who could have made a fortune, but in his tumble-down workshop would create beautiful wheelback chairs for friends at a low price.

In 1910 Gertrude Robins, a famous Edwardian actress living at Moseley Lodge at the time, wrote and produced a play in the old barn, using villagers in the cast, and famous literary critics, including G. K. Chesterton, came down and wrote about it in the national press. From then on drama played an important part in the life of the village and over the years they were successful under the guidance of several qualified drama teachers, including Fanny Dowson, a teacher at R.A.D.A. who once took the current team back stage to meet Sybil Thorndike (related to Fanny by marriage). Until recently there was a strong W.I. drama group, often winning a cup in W.I. Drama Festivals.

High on the Chilterns, midway between London and Oxford, not far from Windsor and the Thames beauty spots, Naphill has a lot to commend it; we who live here are indeed very fortunate.

# Nash

Nash is a village built on a number of springs and is situated on the outskirts of the new city of Milton Keynes. It has approximately 320 inhabitants.

In the early 1900s water was obtained either from a well in the garden or from the village pumps. There were three pumps and villagers could be seen carrying buckets attached to a yoke around the neck of an older member of the family.

Amateur painters can often be seen with their easels by a small footbridge overlooking the pond by the village green. In the past a woodyard overlooked the green and pond and was well known for miles around. It has gone now and in its place is a riding school with stables and jumps for the horses.

In the early part of the century one of the villagers could almost always be seen in the doorway of her cottage making intricate pillow lace for which Buckinghamshire was so well known.

Modern Nash is home for commuters who work either in London or nearby Milton Keynes.

The village had for many years close association with the members of the Whaddon Chase Hunt which has now been disbanded.

# Nether Winchendon

The village is largely unchanged from its 19th century appearance with few modern buildings and many ancient timber-framed houses, and some of the typical local construction of witchert, an unbaked limestone clay mixture. Many retain the ochre colour traditional in the village.

The village is mentioned in the Domesday Book and for many centuries belonged to the Abbey at Notley close by Thame. Some of the cottages still standing are believed to have been lodging houses for the monks.

The church is largely of the decorated period with evidence of earlier origin. The church clock was installed in 1772 by the generosity of Mrs Jane Beresford, Lady of the Manor. It is unusual in having only one hand. The bells were rehung in 1979 and are

enthusiastically rung every week. The excellent condition of the church reflects the generosity of the Spencer Bernard family and the efforts of the villagers.

The village passed from the ownership of Notley Abbey at the Dissolution of the Monasteries to the Denny family, part of whose house, it is believed, is incorporated in the Manor Farm House. The seat of the present owners, the Spencer Bernard family is Winchendon House, a pretty Elizabethan manor house with interesting additions from the Gothic revival of the late 18th and early 19th centuries. Members of the Spencer Bernard family have been in residence continuously since the late 18th century.

A major event is the village fete which involves most of the villagers in one way or another.

124

# Newton Longville

Although there is evidence of early occupation the recorded history of the village does not begin until the invasion of England by William the Conqueror. Walter de Giffard had provided ships and had also been the sword arm of the Conqueror. He was given much land which included Newton Longville. Walter de Giffard was the founder member of the abbey of Santa Foy in Longueville in Normandy. Before he died in 1104 he endowed the abbey with his land in Buckinghamshire to his son, also named Walter de Giffard. He was to found an alien priory or cell in Neutone subordinate to the abbey in Longueville on condition that the prior would send monks to Neutone to build a church and teach the inhabitants of the village. The name Longueville was added then. A pension of £1.6.9d was ordered to be paid to the abbey in Longueville by the priory at Neutone. After the suppression of the priory this was paid to New College, Oxford and is paid to the present day.

Our village was once very small. In 1841 there were 110 houses with a population of 475 and 7 ale houses. The industry then was farming with lace making and plait. Now our village is large with a population of about 2,500. We have a flourishing brickyard and because of our nearness to the railway, many villagers are able to commute each day. With this expansion, most of our ancient buildings have gone. We regret losing our blacksmith's shop which was 800 years old. We had a dove cote which was the only timbered one in the county, and old thatched houses, but with progress we now have water from taps instead of pumps and wells, and gas and electricity instead of open fires, street lights and buses. Memories of the old village are sweet and still remain with many old inhabitants.

# North Crawley

A country lane, an old thatched cot,
Fields, woods and garden plots:
Those lovely elms and chestnuts grand,
And oaks – the finest in the land.

The church so grand with lovely steeple
That is so grand to many people.
The chapel, too, is rather nice,
Where every Sunday folk rejoice.

You'll find the Grange and Rectory there,
Whose architecture is quite rare –
There built among those lovely trees
In spacious parks so nice and green.

Also the pubs, they number three –
The Chequers, Castle, Cock they be –
Where after each day's work is done,
Man has a drink he thinks he's won.

Town Land, too, is also there,
Where lots of people toil and swear.
But of the crops I know are grown
Are among the finest ever known.

So hasten the day when I will be
Back to that village o'er the sea.
Returning home, my duty done,
To a better England we have won.

This poem was written by a North Crawley soldier serving in Burma in the Second World War.

There is a little difference in the village since those days. The Castle Inn is now a residence and the Congregational Chapel as well, although it is pleasing to see that the sign on the front gable, Congregational Chapel 1821, has been left.

Town Land is also still there as an allotment, but before the war there was a waiting list for plots on this allotment, now only about twelve are worked, the remainder have been taken over by a market gardener.

The old thatched cottages, or rather most of them, are still there, and still look nice and tidy, several of them being re-thatched recently.

Those lovely elms, of course, have gone, victims of the Dutch Elm Disease, but the chestnuts have grown into lovely trees, and in the spring when in flower look really beautiful. Lots of new trees have been planted, but, of course, they will be for a future generation to see and admire.

The church, at one time, apparently, did have a steeple, but it became unsafe so was taken down. It is of course the oldest building in the village, dating back to the 11th century.

The Crawley Grange, sad to say, has been vacated by 'The Squire'. It is still there, but has been divided into four separate residences.

# North Marston 🌿

In the year 1290 a rector came to take charge of the parish having previously been priest of the parish of Princes Risborough. This man, the now famous Sir John Schorne, was renowned for his extreme piety. He blessed the village well, known to this day as Schorne Well, thus giving it miraculous healing power to all sick people who drank the water. Much ado was made of this so that many came from far and wide to drink from this well. On the summit of Oving, about a mile away where five ways meet, there was until comparatively recent times a finger board pointing to the direction of the well for guidance of the pilgrims who came to the village to drink the water and visit Sir John Schorne's shrine in St Mary's Church. This finger board read 'To Sir John Schorne's Well'.

Sir John Schorne was incumbent of North Marston from 1290 to 1314 and it was during the years following his death until 1478 that the biggest influx of pilgrims was recorded. As well as increasing the population this also increased the value of the rector's stipend. The Dean of Windsor, Richard Beauchamp, became envious and being one of the patrons of the Church, he obtained permission from the Pope to remove the shrine containing John Schorne's bones and to place it in St George's Chapel, Windsor, where he thought that the pilgrims would come. This proved not to be the case however and so the pilgrimages ceased: the spell had been broken.

A story about the pious Rector, which is famous but ridiculous, is that he conjured the Devil into a long boot and imprisoned him there. However, the laces broke and the Devil escaped. Several well known inns, one at Winslow, have been named after this doubtful episode, 'The Devil in the Boot'.

> 'Sir John Schorne
> Gentleman borne
> Conjured the Devil into a Boot'

The remains of another famous personage are buried in the chancel of St Mary's church, those of John Camden Nield who was a miser and a bachelor. In his will he left a huge legacy to Queen Victoria who, in 1854 and in appreciation, restored the chancel of St Mary's church and filled the east window with stained glass, the subject of which is the Ascension of Christ. The Queen then commanded that Nield be buried beneath the altar steps.

Of the miserly ways of this eccentric, many stories are told. When walking to Winslow he once found that the road was deep in flood following heavy rain. He asked a labouring man to carry him through for payment of a penny, to be paid on reaching the other side. On reaching the half-way through point the man thought well to claim his wage, because he suspected that a haggle over the penny would take place after he had carried Nield through. Nield objected but the man insisted or he would drop his burden in mid-stream. Nield had no alternative but to pay!

The Enclosure Act of 1778 deprived the poor of the parish of their common grazing rights. In lieu of these rights two fields known as Clockland and Poors Piece were dedicated as allotments. All 26 acres of these two fields were cultivated by hand, each man having the tenancy of about two roodes. What each man grew was a big part of a family's livelihood.

The rents of these allotments were collected annually and provided for coal and blankets to be given to the poorer families at Christmastime. Part of the rent of the field 'Clockland' went towards the payment of the winding of the church clock, hence its name.

This ancient charity still operates today, but instead of coal and blankets, groceries are given to the senior citizens at Christmas and a sum is donated towards their annual outing.

# Oakley

Oakley is a small village of some 1300 inhabitants, situated at the foot of Brill hill between Thame and Bicester on the B4011. Many years ago it was almost surrounded by woodland and forests which were used by royalty to hunt wild boar – hence the name Boarstall, our adjoining village, from as early as Saxon times. Oakley is mentioned in the Domesday Book as 'Acheleia' and later records call it 'Ockley'.

There are many interesting houses in the village including the Elizabethan College Farm House which has a wealth of old beams and an unusual open inglenook fireplace upstairs. Oakley House used to be a hunting lodge and was rebuilt as it is today in 1660 after being burned down. It has some very interesting stone mullion windows. The Paddock Cottage has the round back of the old bread oven showing on the outside wall. Manor Farm is a very imposing farmhouse overlooking the Nap with its moat opposite the church. Hedges Farm was built in the late 17th century in red and blue bricks and has a wealth of interior beams. The Old Cottages dates also from the 17th century and was converted from three cottages. The beamed ceilings are very low and the house also features some large open fireplaces. In the centre of the village there is The Old Forge dated 1892. There have been many modern developments and numerous old cottages have been restored and enlarged.

The general appearance of the village changed enormously due to the scourge of Dutch elm disease which left Oakley very open and flat. However the chestnuts around the church and the Manor are a pleasure to all. Sadly the Sequoia tree in the old vicarage garden which had been a landmark for miles around was destroyed by lightning in 1985.

Our church is a very charming and peaceful place despite being on the main road. It has been developed over many centuries, the Nave being 12th century, the north aisle, chancel, sanctuary and south transept early 14th century, various windows are 15th and 16th century and a modern porch has been added on the south door.

The chief form of industry in the past was agriculture, but now most people seek their fortune in Oxford, Aylesbury, Bicester and London.

The hide-out of the notorious Great Train Robbers of the 1960s is Oakley's rather dubious claim to fame. Situated on the outskirts of the village, Leatherslade Farm was very well hidden on a lonely hillside up a narrow track, the house completely surrounded by trees. Now the big elms have all gone and the building can be seen from the main road.

The robbers took up residence some three months before the robbery and used the village stores for some of their supplies. The padlocking of the track gate onto the road immediately after the robbery gave the only clue to their whereabouts.

The peace of the village is threatened today by the proposed extension of the M40 motorway, which it is planned to run within 1½ miles of the village centre.

# Olney

Olney, at the very north of the county of Buckinghamshire, retains its old world charm despite an increase in population due to the expansion of nearby Milton Keynes.

Olney is famous for its pancake race run on Shrove Tuesday from the market place to the parish church of St Peter and St Paul, whose lofty 180 ft spire is a well known landmark. The popular hymn *Amazing Grace* was written by John Newton, the ex-slave trader, when curate of Olney as part of the Olney Hymns, in conjunction with the poet William Cowper who lived here from 1767 to 1786.

The poet's house on the market place is now a museum containing the artifacts of Cowper and Newton as well as housing a collection of hand-made pillow lace, once an important cottage industry here, but now revived as a hobby/craft.

Today Olney has become the sort of place people like to wander around for an afternoon out. It has numerous antique shops, reproduction furniture showrooms, a good bookshop as well as the museum.

# Padbury

The coming of the railways made Padbury important. London could be reached by train via Bletchley in an hour and a half, this comparing very favourably with present day services. A Mr Ambler was Station Master for over 50 years, presiding over his kingdom with great dignity. One wonders what he would have thought now that 'his station' has been demolished and a pleasant housing estate built there. Each morning milk-floats from the surrounding farms gathered at the station, bringing churns of milk which were put on the 'milk train' en route for London. The drivers of the floats were the link between the village and the outlying farms, taking back all the local news, papers and even shopping.

A local carrier, Mr Albert Morris, went to Buckingham weekly with his horse and cart and brought back necessaries for the village folk. Mr Madkins went daily round the local villages also with his horse and cart taking household goods, needles, cottons, laces, etc. while his sister, Miss Mary Ann Madkins made boiled sweets which she sold from their thatched cottage near the station. These were the only sweets obtainable in the village and so were very popular.

As the railways declined Padbury still retained its position of importance as the road at the other end of the village started to carry more traffic, including the local bus service from Aylesbury through Buckingham to Northampton. In recent years the traffic has increased considerably, carrying traffic between London and the Midlands. The main road through the village itself has also become very busy partly because of the building of the new city of Milton Keynes only twelve miles away.

In common with many other villages the occupation of the residents has changed over recent years. Agriculture formerly provided most of the work, there being at least fifteen farms of which most of the houses and cottages belonged to All Soul's College, Oxford. Farms have now been amalgamated and the farm houses sold off. Farm buildings such as barns and even cow sheds have been sold and turned into houses. As a result very few people work on the land, now commuting to places like Milton Keynes, Buckingham University and even going daily to London.

Even with these changes the continuity of village life goes on. Padbury Benefit Society has been in being for many years and in spite of social security and the National Health Service seems to go from strength to strength. The sight of a local band led by the

Society Banner proudly held aloft by its Standard Bearer on its way to the special church service on a Sunday evening in May and parading the village on the Monday, before culminating in a very well-attended dinner held in the Village Hall is surely a sign of the continuity of village life in Padbury.

# Penn Street 🌿

Penn Street is situated on the south of the road between High Wycombe and Amersham near Penn Wood.

Penn House in the village is the home of Lord and Lady Howe and is surrounded by gardens, park and farmlands. Penn House Estates are the principal land owners in the village, which includes Penn Street farm. Grove House, which stands in the grounds, is the old coach house and has the original archway to the stables which are now garages.

Holy Trinity Church built in 1849 has many connections with the Howe family. It is thought likely that the building of the church came from a suggestion made by Queen Adelaide who, when she was visiting Penn House, said it would be an idyllic setting. She used to rest under an oak tree which is now in the church car park and is still called Queen Adelaide's Oak by the villagers. The church has an octagonal tower and 150 ft spire built of oak shingle. The flag from the flagship of Sir William Howe, commander of the British Fleet which defeated the French Fleet off Brest in 1794 hangs in the chancel. When King Edward VII visited Penn House he worshipped in the church and a brass plaque commemorates the fact.

# Penn & Tylers Green 🌿

The area of the continuous villages of Penn and Tylers Green was once the centre of a flourishing tiling industry, whose products provided flooring for many local churches, and also parts of Windsor Castle and the Palace of Westminster.

Nothing of this can now been seen — apart from the odd tile fragment which villagers still might encounter while digging in the garden, and various 'dells' whence clay was dug; — even the tiles from the floor of Penn Church have been moved to the Herts County Museum at St Albans, and we are only reminded of the mediaeval tilers by the names of Tylers Green, Potters Cross and Clay Street.

In the 14th century, tiles were replacing beaten earth for floors, and were produced in many areas, but it is suggested that what made the Penn tiles so sought-after was a technique, possibly introduced by one 'Simon the Payver' of burning glazed floor tiles patterned in two colours – at a price that could undercut other producers. Because of the difficulty in transporting these tiles, the area they were used in was fairly local, but Hedsor wharf on the Thames was accessible by track, and as well as satisfying local customers, the tiles could be despatched even as far as Cobham in Kent, to London and to Windsor.

There used to be a large house at Tyler End Green overlooking the Common, close to Widmer Pond. In 1680, Nathaniel Curzon bought 'the capital messuage at or near Tiler End Greene with its outhouses, stables, yards, gardens and backsides' together with 48 acres, for £477, 'being the greatest price they could get'. Included in the 48 acres were 4 acres immediately adjoining the house running from where The Red Lion and Bank House now stand down to French Meadow Cottage.

Edmund Burke, an Irishman, was a Member of Parliament elected for Wendover under the patronage of Ralph, second Earl Verney, and he was a clever writer and a brilliant talker and deeply involved in all the great issues of his day. In 1794, aged 65, he retired from Parliament to Gregories. In the same year Tylers Green House had been leased to the Government who urgently needed accommodation for a large number of French priests, refugees from the French Revolution. Burke considered the house totally unsuitable for that purpose but was desperate to find somewhere to set up a school for French boys, sons of men who had been killed in the Emigre Corps or still on active service. He set out his proposal for such a school in the house at Penn to the Prime Minister, William Pitt. He described the plight of the poor children living in the squalor of the back streets of London so vividly that Pitt agreed to the scheme and its financing and Burke was made responsible for setting up the school at Tylers Green House to house 60 boys.

After the restoration of the French Monarchy in 1814 it was

taken over by the French Government but closed in 1820. Two years after the School was closed, the house was sold by auction, pulled down and carried away.

Penn and Tylers Green is now better known as the area from which commuters set off on their daily journey to work in the London area; the state of the tracks to Hedsor and the height of the river Thames are of no interest to them – what counts now is the fate of the British Rail trains to Marylebone and the current roadworks and traffic hazards to be encountered on the M40, the A40 and the M25!

# Pitstone ✍

Pitstone was a very small village until the advent of the Tunnel Cement Company in the late 1940s. The company quarries chalk from land to the south west of the village and uses it in the manufacture of cement. This provided employment and more houses were soon needed to house the influx of cement workers.

The area of houses and shops which is always referred to as Pitstone is in fact Pitstone Green. Pitstone itself consists of about fifty houses grouped near Pitstone church half a mile to the south west of Pitstone Green.

Pitstone is proud to boast the oldest surviving post-mill in the country. The mill dates back to 1624, according to documentary references and has been reconstructed from the timbers of the original mill. The mill is owned by the National Trust and was restored by the local history society.

The mill stands on land owned by the Hawkins family of Pitstone Green Farm, who have farmed this land continuously since 1808. Some of the farm buildings house the Pitstone Green Farm Museum which exhibits rural and domestic bygones, farm implements and machinery and details of local history and archaeological finds.

# Prestwood 🌿

'We are the Prestwood nitwits . . .' This saying underlies the belief that this was a community with more than its fair share of 'simpletons'. Until the coming of the railway to Great Missenden in 1892, the people lived in houses straggled and isolated on top of their hill, and there was much inter-marriage.

Prestwood Blacks grew abundantly and competition was very keen to be able to climb the highest tree and fill the most baskets with the cherries which were then taken to Aylesbury and sold for threepence to sixpence a pound. Rivalry was high between two men, Will Peedle and Rupert Taylor, and every June, Will, at the top of the biggest tree, could be heard singing *Little Boy Blue* and boasting afterwards that his voice had been heard all over Prestwood. There was a yearly feast of cherry pies given freely by the orchard owners to all the villagers.

Denner sandstone and flints can still be found in many cottage paths, and were both incorporated with brick in the building of the dwelling houses. The flint stones were collected in baskets by the women and they were paid sixpence for a yard. The flints were also used for filling holes which appeared in the muddy track – the Straight Bit as it was called (now known as the High Street). The stone cutters wore goggles and sacks around their shoulders to keep out the cold and the wet.

From the beech wood the bodgers fashioned chair legs, whilst the women made lace which was sold to travelling pedlars, and plaited straw for the Luton hat trade.

At the turn of the century, Peggie Neal, perhaps one of the first multi-business tycoons – was a bookie's runner, sold hog puddings and castrated cats, first restraining them head first up his sleeve!

After dark, it is notoriously difficult to get horses to pass the corner of one lane. A lady, holding her head in her hands, gallops on a white horse over the uplands and round by Stoney Green Hall; and a wandering disconsolate spirit of some former tenant of Moat Farm seeks the hoard of guineas which were discovered in a wall and appropriated by those engaged in the work of repair.

The first school was opened in 1850 shortly after the consecration of the church which heralded the first Ecclesiastical Parish. In 1900 the headmistress was Miss Margaret McVicar who was a strict disciplinarian and much hated by the children. When she left, some of the boys smeared the gate posts with mud so that her skirts would be dirtied as she passed through them for the last time! In 1909 Moat Lane school opened, one of the first provided by the new Local Education Authorities.

In the Second World War, evacuees came from London. Mrs Harding had two little girls and occasionally, after a bad raid on London, the families, sometimes as many as ten, would come down for a night or two and sleep anywhere in her house. These two girls were very fond of cherries and they put their stones in the garden by the kitchen window – today a fine cherry tree flourishes there!

It is on record that the W.I. made 1,400 lbs of jam in 1942, and also made camouflage nets, collected soap which they sent to liberated France and mending kits to Holland.

When Clement Attlee was Prime Minister he was very fond of entertaining at Chequers and when he left office in 1951 he bought Cherry Cottage in Prestwood. Later when he took the title of Earl Attlee his son became Viscount Prestwood.

No longer is Prestwood a small village of cherry trees, fields and woods – now 6,000 people live here – very many commuting to London. But even so, one has only to walk a short distance in any direction to recapture the past.

# Princes Risborough ⚘

Princes Risborough lies at the foot of the westward escarpment of the Chiltern Hills, in the Vale of Aylesbury. In 1086 it was called Ris(e)Berg, by 1130 altered to Risenberg, then Risebergh or Rysenberg, before the present day spelling. It is recorded that the manor of Princes Risborough was held by Earl Harold, who became the last Saxon King, killed at the Battle of Hastings. Edward III granted the manor to his son the Black Prince, rumoured as having a palace near St Mary's church, thus adding the 'Princes' to its name. Behind the church there still remains a small water-filled section of a moat. On the hillside beyond is the figure of the Whiteleaf Cross, cut into the turf and showing the chalk beneath.

The present 17th century Manor House is a tenanted National

Trust property, with a Jacobean staircase. The earliest record of a dwelling on the site is of a Hall, in 1200. The house, first mentioned in 1589 and at that time called Brooke House, was given by Elizabeth I to Thomas Crompton, together with the whole manor of Risborough. Later it reverted to the Crown. In 1628 Charles I gave the manor and house to the City of London to pay his debts. The house was owned by Sir Peter Lely, the artist, in 1671, and eventually it came into the possession of the Rothschild family who gave it to the National Trust in 1925. The Literary Institute in the High Street, was also owned by the Rothschilds and given to the village in 1891.

Close by the Manor is the former old vicarage, a 16th century cottage with a massive chimney, called Monks Staithe, once the home of Amy Johnson, the aviator, and also of the authoress, Denise Robins.

The Market House, built on brick arches and wooden pillars, topped by a turret, clock and weather-vane, was built in 1824 — a little War Memorial is situated beneath the overhanging ground floor roof. On Saturdays a market stall displays fruit and vegetables and on Thursday mornings from Easter to Christmas the W.I. Market have craft and produce stalls. The Royal charter of Henry VIII entitled a weekly market and two annual fairs, in May and October to be held, which are still held in the Market Square and Church Street. A roundabout, big wheel and stalls crowd the area on fair days.

The picturesque old library in Church Street is a 16th century Wealden house, listed as one of the county's buildings of historic and architectural interest, with black and white timbering to the jettied upper storey, and brick ground floor. Protected by a glass panel inside, a section of the wattle and daub construction is on view. A new brick library is built at the opposite end of the High Street.

The original Norman church founded in the 11th century on the site of St Mary's parish church was completely rebuilt in the 13th, and much altered in Tudor times. During Victorian restoration the new font was installed, and sadly the old font was used as a horse trough and eventually lost.

St Teresa's Roman Catholic church was built in 1937 in modern Byzantine style, in a trefoil shape, with a central dome surmounted by a cross. Attached to the church is the Ker-Maria Convent and home for the aged. The Baptists formed into a church in Risborough in 1701, the present building dates from 1814, modern rooms being added later. The Methodist church was built in 1869 and modernised in recent years.

Until recently there was one main road through the village, but a new layout with roundabouts by-passes the High Street, and takes through traffic from High Wycombe to Aylesbury and Thame.

In recent years there have been many private houses built, the population exceeds 9,000, but many old thatched, timbered and brick and flint houses remain, and whilst cows are no longer driven down the main street, a farm still exists in the village centre behind the Market Square.

# Quainton 🐝

Situated on the southern flank of hills, the centre of the village is the green with its stone cross which is thought was a preaching cross erected in Saxon times before the church was built. A prominent feature is the windmill designed and built by a local man, James Anstiss, in 1830–2. It was built without scaffolding from the inside, floor by floor, with clay bricks baked nearby, and the sails were driven by an engine. It has been unused since 1881, but is now gradually being restored.

The local historian, George Lipscomb, was born in Quainton in 1773 and lived at Magpie Cottage on the west side of the green. After studying medicine in London, he moved back to the village and began his *History of Antiquities of the County of Buckingham*. At first he had a long list of subscribers backing him but gradually the cost of collating the material and travelling round the county used up his money. After the publication of the first volume, he continued writing in poverty and sadly his life ended in 1846 in the debtors' prison.

On Christmas Eve 1752 the villagers gathered on the lawn to witness the budding of the hawthorn which was said to have grown from a shoot off the famous Glastonbury thorn. This holy thorn was reputed to bud each year on Christmas Eve and to bloom on Christmas Day. Earlier in that year Parliament adopted the Gregorian reform of the Julian calendar and the villagers sought proof that Parliament had no power to remove 11 days. The thorn showed no sign of budding, proving the next day was not Christmas Day. So they shunned the festivities and church events were held on the old Christmas Day, January 5th.

Today there is a choice of 4 pubs in the village in which to discuss the day's events. Before the Second World War there were seven pubs and the population was a lot less then! In those days too there were five grocers shops, a drapers and three bakers. On Sundays villagers would take their joints to the bakers in a baking tin with the Yorkshire pudding in a jug to be poured round the meat, and a tin of dripping for the roast potatoes. On Saturdays their cakes would be baked for them and they could buy raw dough, take it home and work fruit, sugar and an egg into it to make dough cake.

One of the greatest attractions for enthusiasts is the Bucks Steam Railway Centre, situated at Quainton Station. They now have a large collection of restored engines and carriages and at weekends short rides can be undertaken in these, complete with hooting engines and the reminiscent smell of wafting steam.

In earlier times, horse racing in the meadows adjacent to The Strand (so named because the bustle of people was likened to the

London Strand) was a local feature and a report of the races in August 1706 describes the large crowds arriving in every sort of conveyance. The green was covered with booths and there was a man in the stocks, covered with slime after a ducking in the nearby pond, having tried to cheat a farmworker of his change. Many of England's nobility were amongst the thousands gathered and Petty Constables were on the look-out for known pickpockets and troublemakers. It was hoped that Queen Anne would visit the races one day as she was rumoured to be interested in establishing a course at 'a place called Ascot'. The Winchendon Mile was the first race and the prize was a plate worth 50 guineas.

Today most of the villagers work either in Aylesbury or in and around the village, with a few commuting to London.

# Radnage 🌿

Radnage is an ancient village, set on the edge of the Chiltern hills.

The church on its picturesque site dates from 1120. The mural paintings are 13th century. The list of rectors dates from 1231. There is a charity of land and investments which brings in an income of approximately £5,000 a year: a third to the church, a third to the church school and a third to the village people.

In the past the main occupations were wood turning and farming. Today it is just farming. Beating the bounds is a tradition still carried out, as is maypole dancing at the school.

The village still retains some old oak beamed and thatched cottages, old country lanes, beechwoods and miles of footpaths.

It is reputed that the ghost of a highwayman goes along the old coach road from London to Oxford and has been sighted in Bottom Road, Radnage, which was part of that road. A ghost in the early 1900s proved to be one of the rector's daughters wrapped in a sheet. She was eventually caught by the local lads.

# Seer Green 🌿

The village is situated amid the leafiest lanes in south Bucks, but on a map made in Norman times it is shown as a hamlet called 'Sere'.

Legend says that Merlin, King Arthur's seer, rested here on his journeys to and from Camelot. There is a well in the village which still bears his name, and it was here that the villagers came to consult him about the future – hence the name 'Seer Green'.

History tells us that Edward, the Black Prince, built a lodge here, and he and his courtiers hunted the deer which abounded in the surrounding forests of beech, oak and elm. The lodge, now named Hall Place, is still a well preserved place of residence.

A lady, who was born and has lived all her life in Seer Green can remember when in the centre of the village there was a large cherry orchard from which the fruit was harvested and taken to London by horse and van. Each year a festival was held for which housewives made cherry pies in the shape of a small pasty, and these were cooked by the local baker, Mr Lofty, in the large bread ovens. People came from many miles for this event and Seer Green became known as the cherry pie village. In recent years a Cherry Pie Fayre has been held at the local school at which cherry pies are still sold. Mr Lofty would also bake Christmas cakes made by the housewives and on Christmas Day would heat his ovens to cook chickens for the festive day.

The village wells were the only source of drinking water and here the men met for a smoke and a chat whilst drawing their daily supplies.

Nearly every house had chickens and perhaps a pig in the back garden and in the autumn children were sent to collect acorns to feed the pigs during the winter.

There was a village 'snob', Mr Loveday, for whom the children would collect boots and shoes to be mended, and deliver them back to their owners – some as far afield as Jordans – for which they were paid the princely sum of one penny (old currency) a basket.

Lace making was taught in the Baptist Church Sunday school hall, and the Seer Green pattern became the motif for many beautiful pieces of work.

With the coming of the railway in the 1920s, the village grew in size and the population is now in the region of 3,000.

# Shabbington 🦡

Shabbington is a pretty village situated on a rounded hill above the river Thame, which divides the two counties, Buckinghamshire and Oxfordshire. A hundred years ago it was an outlying part of the Waterperry Estate, when the farms and cottages were sold off at that time. There are about 8 farms that were mainly rich pasture land, but quite a few fields are arable now.

The character of the village has altered a lot in recent times. There used to be many thatched cottages. Some remain, having been renovated, but a lot were demolished and modern houses built on the sites. In the 1950s and 1960s we had several estates erected off different roads, which have proved very beneficial to the village.

Hundreds of years ago, we had an abbey in the field near the church. No trace of it remains but the outlines of the fishponds they used can still be traced close by the river.

At one time there was a watermill close to the river bridge and the river was diverted to send the water to turn the wheel. There still is the waterfall at that point, recently renovated and probably about 8 ft high.

We were fortunate in having a sewerage scheme put into the village in the 1890s, which was very foreseeing on someone's part and it was built so well that it has been very little altered since. For years, drinking water was fetched from the village pump in the centre. It was sparkling spring water and it was carried by a yoke and big buckets. This was an entertainment in itself as lots of people were there and all the news was soon passed round. This was all finished in the 1930s, when the mains water came. The old lamps were also thrown out at that time when electricity was installed.

We have always been fortunate in having a village stores and Post Office, which now is a wonderful meeting place. We have a small village hall, erected in 1929, which is ideal for meetings and children's parties, but for concerts and wedding receptions, we go to the larger halls in neighbouring villages.

Money was scarce in the 1920s. Farmers had probably a dozen men working and others walked miles and miles for employment, did a good days work and then had to walk home again. The cottage ladies found employment in the larger houses and some walked the 3½ miles to Thame to work in the houses there and in the schools. They would wear long hessian aprons in the mornings and lovely white aprons in the late afternoon and evenings.

The farms are now run mainly by the farmers and their families, and the villagers find employment in commuting long distances in their cars.

A wonderful pageant was held at Long Crendon Manor in 1922. The east window of the church was in danger of falling out and had to be shored up. The pageant was held – everyone dressed up in period costume and crowds of people attended – the money rolled in and was enough to rebuild the east window.

Shabbington is a very caring village and a very pleasant place to spend a lifetime.

# Skirmett ✒️

It was the Danes in the 9th century who first settled in the valley, discovering it as they travelled up the Thames. They are thought to have named the place from two words 'shire' and 'meeting place'.

The hamlet of Skirmett today is a row of 55 houses and cottages along a stream at the bottom of a valley. There are a number of outlying farms on the hills and one in the village. The road runs along the length of the valley starting at Lane End and going down into the valley before joining the villages of Fingest, Frieth, Turville, Skirmett and Hambleden. In former times the hamlet of Skirmett was an offshoot of Poynants Manor.

The houses are a mixture of old and new. Many of the buildings have changed their uses as the chapels have become houses, as have the bakery, shop and school. Only a third of the people work in the area. The village does not serve as a centre as it once did but still has two public houses and a village hall.

# Slapton ✒️

Within living memory Slapton was a self contained village with three farms, a brickyard, church and chapel, school, shop, mill, a blacksmith, cobbler, baker and brewer. The rector lived in a gracious house set in large grounds.

Today the village is luckier than most as it still has a post office stores, a school for the younger children, a pub and a church. The farms remain too, but the Maltings are used by the publican as a store.

The church remains steadfast, standing every spring-time in a sea of cowslips watching over the community as it has done since 1223. The name of Turney is a village name to this day and many of the gravestones, lichened and leaning, carry the surnames of today's villagers, reflecting the continuity of village life, despite the much talked about influx of townies and commuters.

Most of the inhabitants are commuters these days as there is very little work within the village boundaries. So the village is a quiet place during the day as people go far afield to earn their living, many travelling to London from nearby Cheddington station. However, despite the daily exodus, the village is a thriving place with organisations catering for all age groups.

Rising crime rate in rural areas was responsible for the formation of a Village Watch Scheme which has now become Neighbourhood Watch now that these schemes are official in the county. This has increased our community spirit making us all more aware of one another. 1986 marked our first entry into the Best Kept Village competition.

The village administers its own charity which has been in existence for 400 years and is named after Sir Thomas Knyghton, a former Rector of Holy Cross Church. The charity books record the giving of shoes, petticoats, wood for the fire, tools to learn a trade, weekly sick benefits, money for learning to sing the psalms, and – ultimately – a coffin to the poor and needy. There is not such obvious poverty today but the Trustees continue the caring work mindful of the example set by their predecessors.

There are ghosts of course, what village would be complete without them? An old lady, dressed in black and carrying a basket wanders along the route of a defunct footpath; the moonlight glints on the buckles of a Rector's shoes, all that can be seen of him as he rushes to an ancient affray; a young girl runs in one direction and her horse gallops in another as they search endlessly for one another and in one of the old cottages children cry.

The *Northamptonshire Mercury* records the trial of a witch on July 2nd 1770. She was to have been tried by water ordeal and weighing against the Bible at the mill in Slapton but the miller declined to carry out the trial before so many spectators, but promised to do it later in private.

# Soulbury ✤

Soulbury overlooks the Ouzel Valley and consists of several half-timbered and thatched houses around a green, and an attractive church dating back to the 14th century. The village comprises of some 210 houses at present, the most notable of these being Lovetts Charity School House, built in 1724.

There are two manor houses in the parish of Soulbury, Chelmscote Manor and Liscombe Park. Liscombe Park which is large and rambling and was built in the 16th century is set behind imposing gates on the Soulbury-Leighton Buzzard road. The Lovetts, who used to be Lords of the Manor here have a fine memorial in the Parish Church.

Robert Lovett left to the poor of Soulbury the sum of £300.00. This amounted to £540.00 when interest was added and was used to teach twenty four boys and girls a trade. The interest is now divided among the children of the village aged 12 and 18 who are in full time education to cover the costs of uniform, tuition and travel.

Soulbury used to be a farming community with the little hamlet of Hollingdon close by. However, over recent decades it has gradually become more of a commuter suburb with many residents working in London and the evergrowing Milton Keynes.

Traffic is an increasing problem in the village as many pass this way to get to Milton Keynes. A planned by-pass around Leighton Buzzard, the nearest big town, should alleviate the problem when eventually built.

Soulbury does not have ghosts and headless horsemen, but has a stone situated on Chapel Hill which is reputed to roll down Chapel Hill every night when it hears the clock strike 12 o'clock.

# Speen 🌿

The village of Speen lies 600 ft up in the Chilterns and is in the parish of Lacey Green and Loosley Row. At one time the village was referred to as Uphill, but in the Land Survey of 1823 was given the name of Speen.

At the time of William the Conqueror's Domesday Book there were only 5 or 6 dwellings in the area of Speen, but during the 16th, 17th and 18th centuries more houses and inns were built, and several of these houses are still in use today. These lovely old buildings contribute to the charm of the village as do the brick and flint houses built in the early 19th century, when people were allocated plots of land at a small charge in exchange for their common rights, when the number of houses increased to 36. However, the village really began to grow after 1950 with the main increase being between 1965–1975. Today there are about 200 houses. Several of the recently built properties have been built in the style of the original brick and flint cottages. The village now has a population of approximately 700.

When the Baptist Church was built in 1802 it became the focal point for the inhabitants, and it continues to play a large part in the life of the village. The church's most important day in the year, Anniversary Sunday, is still held on the second Sunday in July, and each year a Flower Festival and Candlelit Carol Service are held. Many villagers, including non-members of the church, take part in these events, which makes them real 'village' occasions.

The Village Hall, originally built as a Temperance Hall, was bought by the village in 1924 for £125, and became the meeting place for the many clubs which were formed, including a Wireless Club where the men made their own crystal sets or 'cats' whiskers', and a thriving dramatic society. The Hall was modernised in 1970 and in 1986 had a small extension and repairs and improvements.

In the past Speen was a very close knit and industrious community with many cottage industries and smallholdings. Almost everything could be made or bought within the village which had its own shoemaker, tailors, chair-makers, chimney sweep, baker, builders, carpenters and undertaker, wheelwright and ladder maker. Men, known as 'bodgers', worked in shacks or sheds in the

Hampden woods making chair legs for the Wycombe furniture trade, and the villagers could buy a permit for one shilling to collect dead wood and roots for their winter fuel. The women churned butter and cured their own bacon, and made most of the products needed for their families. Lace-making was one of the thriving cottage industries. In the 1800s there was a lace-making school in a flint and brick cottage now called The Roses, and girls started to learn the art at the age of 3. Miss Dawson of the old

Bakehouse taught lace-making in the district until her retirement in 1985, and there is still a great interest in lace making in the village. Miss Dawson was awarded the O.B.E. in 1985 for her services to lace-making.

To-day, apart from farmers, and local builders who live in the village, the only industries carried on are the Speen Pottery, Speen Spinners and Weavers, and the Stained Glass Studio at Piggotts Hill.

The rest of the Speen residents either work in neighbouring towns or commute to London.

Like so many old villages, Speen is said to have a ghost. A highwayman, Mr Cooper, is said to be buried with his treasure in Highwood Bottom, where a stone marks the burial spot. People are said to have seen the ghost of Cooper roaming the lane, and children used to be told to hurry home 'or the Highwayman would get them'. Some boys once planned to lift the stone to see what lay underneath, but they became scared and ran away.

Speen residents are fortunate to have a fine playing field, thanks to the efforts of the villagers who bought the land in 1935 from Wheelers Wycombe Breweries for the sum of £160. Every year on November 5th there is a huge bonfire and firework display, with soup, hotdogs and doughnuts. And in July, perhaps the highlight of the year, the Speen Fete is held, when every village organisation contributes to the planning and running of the stalls and sideshows and all the villagers join in on the day. It is on these occasions that Speen once again becomes Speen Village.

# Steeple Claydon

The steeple on St Michael's church can be seen as one approaches the village. Many believe mistakenly that Steeple Claydon is so called because of this, but the manor of Stepul Claydone is mentioned in the Domesday Book. The steeple and tower were not built until the mid-19th century.

Calvert clay has a lot to do with the growth of this village for its prosperity came after the brickworks were built. Work on these began in 1898 and production of bricks started in 1900. Today over 500 people work there although at one time the London Brick Company (as it was then) employed over 1,000 people and was the main employer in the district. Although the brickworks are at Calvert, Steeple Claydon became the village which grew around it. The reason being that it was the village with a sewerage system and a piped water supply. The village continues to grow and at the last census taken, had a population of 1,692.

There are five public houses in the village. There is an old jingle about them which goes thus:

'The Black Horse kicked the Crown
and drank the Fountain dry,
The Sportsman shot the Prince of Wales
and made the Phoenix fly'.

The Black Horse has been non-existent for many years, but Bull Lane where it once stood is likely to be remembered, for nearby is a small estate named for obvious reasons Taurus Close.

Many villagers came and settled here after the Second World War when prefabricated bungalows were erected to house the brickworkers, who were given priority on local council housing lists as there was such a demand for bricks to rebuild the bombed towns and cities of Britain, and homes were desperately needed for the ex-servicemen returning home.

At the time, it seemed odd to house brickworkers in aluminium prefabs imported from America, but many were grateful for the accommodation afforded which had every 'mod-con'. These included a hot and cold water system, with bath, and the then ultimate luxury (in the villages anyway) of a fitted kitchen with a refrigerator!

The credit for the growth of the village into the thriving community it now is may be attributed to three local councillors, all now deceased, who had the vision and ambition to improve it. Oddly enough, two of these, Mr Tom Mitchinson and Mr Allan Shaw, originated from the North-East of England. The new school, the third phase of its building still to be completed, was named after county-councillor Shaw. Councillors Tom 'Mitch' as he was affectionately known, and George Beckett worked tirelessly for the village and organized many events to raise money to improve the recreation ground, build a new pavilion and provide a childrens corner.

# Stewkley

Stewkley in the Vale of Aylesbury is the longest village in England, one mile either side of our beautiful and most unspoilt Norman church, St Michaels, which dates back to 1150. This division was known as 'Up-Town' (north) and 'Down Town' (south) and friendly rivalry existed between the two.

Stewkley was mentioned in the Domesday Book and was then spelt 'Steuclai'.

It is recorded that during the Civil War Oliver Cromwell and his soldiers put their horses in Stewkley church when they brought many guns to Pitch Green Hill and put them on three terraces. Also, quite recently a cannon ball was found behind the fireplace of a farm house, which probably dated back to this time.

Village life was mainly focused around the church and chapels and a hundred years ago Stewkley could offer just about every service required. These were six grocers, two butchers, a baker, carpenter, blacksmith, wheelwright, harness maker, shoemaker and ten public houses.

The malting and brewing of beer was carried out in quite a big way on a site which is now called The Malting Yard and some of the beer was taken to London on wagons.

Stewkley was noted for its excellent straw plaiting which was made by men, women and children. It was very well paid. The men could earn 6/- to 12/- a week which was more than for farm work.

Brick making was also an important source of work in the area at The Kiln Dunton Road, and eight cart horses complete with shining brasses used to pass through the village to Swanbourne railway station to collect the coal for firing the bricks.

A tale told by older residents in the village is how, at dusk, boys used to go 'netting sparrows'. They put a net one side of the hedge and 'bashed' the other, then they would kill the birds for sparrow pie.

The Stewkley Feast, 11th October, originated from the Feast of St Michael and on that day all land owners collected their rent and they would give their tenants a meal of roast beef and christmas pudding, and the school children were given two days holiday to enjoy the fun of the fair which came at feast time.

A 16th century cottage, now 14 Ivy Lane, was at one time a

152

forge. From 1912–14 the cottage was the country residence of Mrs Pankhurst and her daughter Sylvia, no doubt many of the leaders of the 'Votes for Women' campaign were visitors here. Soon after Mrs Pankhurst's disappearance from London the whole country was seeking to learn her whereabouts; no one knew she was living in Stewkley.

No record of Stewkley would be complete without the inclusion of the village ghost, in the name of the Rev. William Wadley. 'Old Wadley' haunted the Manor House. It is said he had a long flowing beard and rode a white horse.

Perhaps the 'new' Stewkley grew out of a long and determined fight, in the late 1960s and early 1970s against the siting nearby of London's proposed third airport. Had the Roskill Commission had its way, this Buckinghamshire village would have disappeared from the county map. Once the threat of the airport's arrival had been squashed, newcomers began to settle, and building developments sprang up – clusters of houses, and single buildings, filling in many of the remaining open paddocks along either side of the so called 'straggly' High Street. Many of these 'newcomers' were to be commuters, but have integrated into the existing community assisting with whatever needs to be done to maintain village life.

# Stoke Hammond 🌿

Situated on the main A4146 road between Bletchley and Leighton Buzzard, the road through the village has a constant stream of traffic. Fast-moving cars and heavy articulated lorries thunder through this once sleepy thoroughfare, so much so that a new bypass is scheduled for 1989, when hopefully peace will reign once more in this attractive village.

The village has seen several colourful characters in its time, one being a strange parson. He lived alone in the rambling old rectory adjoining the churchyard, and preferred liquid refreshment to solid. His favourite tipple was whiskey. Villagers would see him walking up the road from the Dolphin Inn carrying an American cloth bag containing a bottle or two! As might be expected, he 'saw', and 'heard', many unusual things. Close to the church the main railway line ran in a cutting, and the reverend gentleman was convinced that engine drivers sent him coded messages on their whistles. The old rectory is said to be haunted, so perhaps this is why he took to the bottle!

Another colourful character was a landlord of the Dolphin Inn. In the days when most householders kept a few backyard hens, a spate of thefts took place. The landlord perpetuated a rumour that certain village boys were probably responsible for the crime. However, he himself was caught in the act of stealing poultry from the owner of Stoke Lodge, who clonked him on the head with a spanner, thus making the thief easily identifiable. Several days later the said landlord was found hanging by his neck from a beam in the loft of the old stables.

The Anglican church was built in the 12th century. It stands on the highest ground in the village, its east window overlooking Great Brickhill. Around the old stone walls the dead of many generations of villagers peacefully lie. An avenue of trees leading to the heavy oak door has recently been replaced with young trees. Perhaps in years to come their branches will meet overhead as the old ones did. Unfortunately there is now no-one to ring the bells. Many years ago an old blind man rang all three. By pulling the ropes with his hands, and with the other attached by a loop to his foot, he managed to call the villagers to worship.

At one time, farming, consisting of dairy herds, sheep, pigs, and poultry, was a main source of employment. Now the land has been sold off into large or small units. Arable, grass-land, and riding horses, are now considered to be more economical ways to farm. And in the days of steam trains, the railway employed a number of men. Young women mostly went into service, or were apprenticed to dressmaking. Today, residents work in a wide variety of occupations, travelling by car to local towns, and to the new city of Milton Keynes.

# Stoke Mandeville

Stoke Mandeville is of course known nationwide for the hospital for spinal injuries. But the village has its own attractions.

The church of St Mary the Virgin is in the heart of the old village. Built in 1866 to replace the even older ruined church in the fields, it stands in a lovingly tended churchyard, surrounded by sweetly scented lime trees. Originally there were five bells; during the time Rev. Winterton was vicar three more were installed. The belfry is now unsafe, so no ringing is heard at present. Inside the simple, cool interior is a monument to Dorothy Brudenell – whose father was once Lord of the Manor. Her likeness is embroidered on the banner of the Stoke Mandeville Women's Institute.

Across the green, part of the ancient Common Land, is the village school. The original part of the building is still in use and bears the date 1898. All the children were taught in the two rooms. Now the much enlarged premises house the County Combined School with almost 300 pupils.

In the past, a grand party took place here each New Year's Eve. The partition between the rooms folded back – the tortoise stove well stoked – tea urn bubbling – home-made cakes and lemonade laid ready – the fun would begin.

To the music of fiddle and piano, all the old dances – Sir Roger – Lancers – Veleta, interspersed with games of trencher, Nuts in May etc. would raise the temperature, and the dust, until everyone was glad to rest. So until midnight, when, outside in the cold night air *Ring out wild bells* would be sung to welcome the New Year.

Manor Cottage next to the school is one of the lovely 18th century cottages and beyond, near the entrance to the allotments, is where the Bell Pond – now regretfully filled in, was situated.

Across the allotments in Marsh Lane is the present-day wheelwright's yard. Most of his work is to keep in repair pony traps and other light vehicles still to be seen occasionally in the lanes.

In Risborough Road, heavy container lorries from the continent and the many fast cars make it difficult to cross! The road here is wide and part of the old common land provides an open green with lovely silver birch trees and the copper beech planted to commemorate the coronation of Queen Elizabeth II. Less than 50 years ago the quiet roads were lined with magnificient elms, and deep ditches either side carried storm water to the ponds and streams.

Round the corner is the 15th century Old Thatch next to The Bull, where in the past much business was transacted over a pint! The three old cottages under one rooftree which stand next, are required to pay the sum of £1 per annum in tithe under the terms of the Jackson Charity dated 1726!

Our hairdresser has a shop opposite the church, where Pargeters general store once supplied most of the villagers' everyday needs in the 1930s. Older residents will remember it being dominated by the wonderful smell – spice, tea, coffee, herbs, polishes, vegetables etc. Sugar and dried goods were weighed on brass scales and put into blue or brown 'made' paper bags.

Children of that era were allowed round the corner of the counter to spend their Saturday pennies. Gob stoppers, sherbert dabs, liquorice and boiled sweets at 4 oz for a penny! Times *have* changed!

# Stokenchurch

Stokenchurch is a hill-top village in the Chilterns, on the Bucks/ Oxon border. The name Stokenchurch is believed to be derived from the 'The Church in the Stocken', that is a church built within a stockade to protect the inhabitants from animals and outlaws.

The earliest part of the church dates from the 12th century and was built of timber and thatch. Hannah Ball who founded the first English Sunday School lived in Mill Road and was buried in the churchyard in 1792.

It had always been an industrious village with five chair factories and three sawmills. Rush and cane seating was done by the women of the village at home. The rush and canes were brought from the river Thames by the Towerton cart. They were soaked in the ponds till used. The children collected the chairs and their mothers were paid 2d a chair. Completed chairs were taken to Oxford and High Wycombe by horse and cart.

Agriculture played a large part in village life as there were 14 farms in the area and a post windmill where grain was taken to be ground. Unfortunately it was blown down in 1926 and only the name of Mill Road remains.

At that time there were two butchers and slaughterers in the village. Stokenchurch suffered from water shortages as there was only one well in the centre of the village, dug by Colonel Fane and John Brown to a depth of 360 ft. Trailers of water were towed round the village by traction engine for the villagers to collect their water in buckets at 1½d each. Later there was a water tower built but was eventually demolished as a military exercise. The village had three wheelwrights and two blacksmiths. One wheelwright was situated where Tower Garage is now, and he was often seen running across the road with an iron rim to cool down in the dew pond opposite. The bakehouse was used during the week for breadmaking and on Sunday lunches were cooked for families at a cost of one dish for one penny, but meat, potatoes and batter would be 1½ d.

A brass band accompanies the Methodist Church Sunday School round the village prior to their sports and games day behind Coopers Court Farm. Stokenchurch also had a dance band and a town crier who walked round the village announcing all forthcoming events. The village had a 'lock-up' where trouble-makers were put up for the night before being taken to Watlington Court the next day.

Lacemaking was done in the doorways on warm sunny days and tambour beading was also popular.

The common land was enclosed in 1861 under the General Closure Act and was reserved for the annual fair and horse sales on the 10th and 11th July. It also provided the village with goods not always available to them, and a service which was 'the extractor of teeth'. Teeth were pulled out for one shilling with a musical accompaniment to drown the yells of pain! In the surrounding woods chair bodgers worked with pole lathes making chair legs and backs for the factories.

When a death occurred in the village a death knell was rung, one for a child, two for a woman and three for a man, and would continue for one hour. There were three undertakers.

Milk was delivered from the farms by horse and float and was measured into the customer's own jug. The children played in the streets with hoops, spinning tops, skipping and marbles.

The village was famous for a local notable; Bartholomew Tipping. A secondary school has been named after him and was founded in 1675 for instructing twelve boys in reading, writing and accounts. He provided a schoolroom and a house for the schoolmaster, clothes for the boys – 'blue coats and breeches'. The house called Tippings is still in the village.

In the 1960s the coming of the M40 changed the character of the village with several housing estates being built when London became a reasonable commuting distance by motorway.

# Stoke Poges 🖋

Stoke Poges is situated between Slough and Gerrards Cross. It is an area made up of several scattered hamlets and comprises estates, woodlands and common land.

In 1086 it was known as Stockes and was the meeting place of the Stoke Hundred (one of the Chiltern Hundreds). In 1291 Robert Poges married Amicia de Stoke and the parish became known as Stoke Poges. Until well into the 19th century the southern boundary was the Bath Road and in 1835 Slough was designated in a topographical dictionary as a hamlet in the parish of Stoke Poges.

St Giles church is remote from the village but situated near the Manor House one and a half miles distant. This was probably firstly a Saxon thane's dwelling then an 'embattled' castle of the 14th century and lastly was the Elizabethan Manor house of the 2nd Earl of Huntingdon. Part of the church is Saxon but it is mostly Norman with the Tudor Hastings Chapel as a later addition.

The churchyard is famous for its connection with Thomas Gray the poet who died in 1771 and who there lies buried with his mother. His *Elegy written in a Country Churchyard* surely one of the best known poems in the English language, is generally supposed to have been written at Stoke Poges as the poet spent much time here with his mother who lived for some years at West End Farm in the village. This, enlarged, became Stoke Court and was the home of the Penn family. It is now the administrative headquarters of an International Pharmaceutical Company and has recently been rebuilt after a disastrous fire in 1979.

Adjoining the churchyard is the National Trust Field where stands the monument to Gray erected in 1799 by John Penn, a grandson of the founder of Pennsylvania. This has been restored after an appeal launched by the late Sir John Betjeman in 1977.

James Wyatt's Gothic vicarage was built in 1802 to replace an earlier building which John Penn had demolished as it spoiled his view from Stoke Park, the house he had built in the late 18th century, the old Manor House having fallen into decay. One wing of this is still standing and is occupied as business premises. Stoke Park House is now the headquarters of the Stoke Poges Golf Club and the surrounding parkland forms the championship Golf Course.

Sefton Park originally known as Stoke Farm was built for Lady Molyneux daughter of the Earl of Sefton. Another well-known person who lived there was Lady de Frece, better known as Vesta Tilley the actress. During the Second World War, the Gordon Highlanders' famous 51st division and American G.I.s were quartered there prior to the invasion of Normandy and were visited by many famous war leaders though it was 'hush hush' at the time. After the war Glaxo Laboratories moved in and there developed the Salk vaccine.

In Rogers Lane is the house known as Uplands, built in 1772 to house a lace factory, later becoming the village workhouse and now a gracious family home.

Not far from the vicarage is the Clock House built in 1765 as almshouses to replace the original Hospital (or Almshouses) founded by Lord Hastings in 1557. The oldest house in the village is an early 16th century timber-framed house also now occupied by a business firm.

As Thomas Gray's poem has it the villagers seem mainly to have kept 'the noiseless tenour of their way', in the past being mostly employed on the land or in service in the large houses. The exception seems to have been at the time of the Enclosures in the early part of the last century when the villagers' rights of grazing their animals on the common were extinguished. Between 1810 and 1814 a great struggle went on in the parish – many of the gentry and villagers joined forces to preserve the right of the poor to gather fuel on 200 of the original 460 acres. This is now designated an 'area of special scientific interest' and is still administered by four elected trustees from the village under the chairmanship of the vicar of Stoke Poges as was agreed at the time of Enclosure.

It is interesting to note that the needy still have help with their fuel bills, paid for from funds derived from charges to Public Authorities for such things as telephone poles, gas pipes laid across the common etc.

In a mysterious *Census of the Poor* of 1832 in the Bodleian Library at Oxford there are reports of the villagers, one being transported for seven years and another 'taken up on suspicion of being concerned in an intended conspiracy to fire the workhouse'.

Folk of good character are mentioned and also men who were 'shady' and 'bosky' i.e. given to drink. Among the craftsmen mentioned are brickmakers, sawyers, wheelwrights, a cordwainer, a smith and an unusual occupation of 'kindler maker'.

At the time of the First World War the population of the village was under 1500 and 48 fell in battle. Now the population is 5,000, made up of all sections of the socio-economic groups who get their livelihoods in London, Slough, Windsor, Heathrow Airport etc. The village contains all types of dwelling and an up to date shopping precinct and although no longer presents an agricultural outlook possesses a strong community spirit.

# Taplow ✤

A settlement at Taplow has been in existence since the Stone Age, as shown by the finding of artifacts of that period. Its name is derived from that of a Saxon chief, Tappa, whose burial mound is evident. Saxon objects have been excavated and these, along with earlier finds, are now housed in the British Museum.

Taplow has remained a village, with its church, school, hall, inn and some old dwelling houses around the green. High above the beautiful stretch of the Thames known as Cliveden Reach, where the river separates Taplow from Maidenhead, is Taplow Court with its well laid out gardens. The original manor house was on this site, the estate was more extensive, including what is today Cliveden estate.

In the grounds of Taplow Court is Bapsey Pond where, it is claimed, St Birinius baptised his followers in Roman times. This is near the burial mound where a service is held at dawn on Easter Day. The church, St Nicolas, stood on the estate until 1828, when it was demolished and rebuilt on its present site in the centre of the village. It is one of several churches served by a team ministry.

The manor house changed in appearance through the ages. In the 17th century it ceased to be Crown property, being sold to Sir William Hampson in the reign of James I. He in turn sold off the part which became Cliveden. It was last renovated by Pascoe Grenfell in 1855 to give it the Gothic appearance we see today. It is now used for industrial prposes. What beautiful surroundings in which to work!

So was established an area of large houses, with a village of cottagers serving the big houses. In the 19th and early 20th centuries there were four shops, a post office and the inn, the Oak and Saw. Conditions in the village have changed – shops and post office have disappeared, but services are infrequent and the railway station, though nearer than originally, sited as it was at the Dumbbell Hotel, is still a distance away. Quite a lot of building has been carried out since the Second World War, the houses mainly occupied by reasonably affluent people who work away from the village, many commuting to the City. The station has always carried commuters to London. In early times noble Lords travelled to the Houses of Parliament, hence the name of Noblemen's Corner. Just after the First World War the local village simpleton noted that they all wore bowler hats. He asked the village bobby whether he too could wear one, and was told that he needed a licence!

The present Cliveden House, the third on the site, was designed by Sir Charles Barry. It was bought from the Duke of Westminster by William Waldorf, later Lord Astor, in 1893. He had the beautiful water gardens laid out. It continued to be lived in by his family until 1966, though the estate had been given to the National Trust in 1942. Before the Second World War Lord Astor's son and daughter-in-law, Nancy, made it the centre for the literary and political society of the day, 'The Cliveden Set'. There were scandalous tales told both at that time and earlier, in Edwardian times, when there was a row of houses let to ladies who frequented the famous Skindles hotel on the riverside.

Stamford University leased part of the house from the National Trust for fourteen years. It is now a very luxurious, expensive hotel.

In the Cliveden estate the Canadian Red Cross Memorial Hospital was built during the Second World War, though in the Great War there had been a hospital unit established there. After the war it became a Health Service hospital until 1984. There was great sadness when it was closed, as it was very much a 'family' hospital.

# The Lee 🌿

The Lee (from the Old English place name 'leah' – a clearing) is situated high amongst beechwoods on the scarp of the Chilterns.

Very much an enclosed village before the advent of the motor car, when agriculture and allied pursuits, such as straw-plaiting, were the means of existence, many things changed when the Liberty family bought the Manor and the greater part of the land between Great Missenden and St Leonards, during the latter part of the 19th century.

The original parish was tiny, and centred on the small 12th century church, served only by visiting priests, first from Missenden Abbey, and then very occasionally after the Reformation. Consequently the village became strongly non-conformist and there were three chapels (Methodist, Baptist, and self-governing Emmanuel). The Methodist chapel and Emmanuel still thrive.

Until 1867 most villagers had to travel to Wendover for 'marrying and burying'. In that year the new church was built, and a chancel added shortly after, through the generosity of the Liberty

family, with oak linenfold panelling made in the Liberty workshops, and interesting art-nouveau lamp holders for the whole church.

Today the village has become a haven for commuters and for those who can work at home. Proximity to London is so advantageous that the price of property has rocketed, and cottages are frequently extended in size, but many of the old dwellings show the traditional brick and flint construction that is a feature of Chiltern buildings. The centre of The Lee is a Conservation Area and the whole is contained in the Chiltern Area of Natural Beauty, so that development has been contained.

Items of interest include the Jubilee Well of 1901. This illustrates the difficulty of water supplies at that time, and until recently. Before the well was sunk cottagers relied on ponds for watering animals, and on rainwater collected in underground tanks, for their own use, when roofs were tiled. When piped water was eventually brought to the village, one farmer, with a herd of Jersey T.T. cows, had water laid on for his precious animals, but did not see any necessity to have a supply of water laid on in his own house!

Another historic landmark is the ship's figurehead at the entrance to Pipers, the home of Mr and Mrs Arthur Stewart-Liberty. This is of Admiral Earl Howe, and was taken from the last of the 'Wooden Walls of England', when it was bought for the timber, and used in the building of the Liberty store in Regent Street, London.

# Thornborough ✎

Thornborough has been a farming community since before the Domesday Book, where it is recorded that in the manor there was land for 11 ploughs, or oxen teams, and a meadow for 4 ploughs. Thornborough parish had two large fields, East or Thornton Field, and West or Padbury Field, divided into strips or furlongs which were a unit of tenure. About 1325 a third field was carved out of these and called Mill Field. This gave a two-year crop rotation for the villagers, followed by a fallow or rest year.

On one of the highest points in the parish is the site of a windmill where corn was ground in the 17th century. The parish is bounded on the west side by the Claydon brook, a tributary of the river Ouse, which is spanned by a medieval bridge with six arches, by-passed now for modern traffic. Close by there are two ancient burial mounds.

In the centre of the village, between the 17th century manor, the village hall and the village school, stands St Mary's church. Parts of the south wall are believed to date from Saxon times, but the earliest records begin in the 12th century. In the floor of the nave, protected by the carpet, lies a fine brass dedicated to John and Isabel Barton. The tower houses a peal of five steel bells, which, after a silence of over thirty years, have been re-hung, and may be heard once more ringing joyously across the fields. The mechanisation of the tower clock brings to an end the labour of love of the verger, who has climbed up the tower by a vertical ladder every day for no less than sixty years to wind up the clock by hand.

The village hall was built in 1846, with money given by the Verney family of Botolph Claydon, for the purpose of teaching the children the scriptures. Incorporated in the hall was a two-bedroom house for the schoolmaster. Up to 126 children were taught in the hall at any one time. After the present school building took its place in 1910, the hall was used, as it still is today, for village functions such as dances and whist drives.

Many of the village families have roots in Thornborough which go back for many generations. Whereas there are now only two public houses and one shop, many of the present-day inhabitants can remember the days when there were several shops and inns. Some 50 years ago, the old bakehouse played an important role in village life. On Sundays at about 10.30 am husbands and a few sons could be seen dressed in their best navy blue serge suits, with white shirt and navy tie, and probably a pork pie hat, wending their way towards the bakehouse. They bore a large tray with the Sunday joint in a meat tin, the Yorkshire pudding mixture, and another dish containing potatoes to be roasted, and also the weekly fruit cake mixture, the whole covered with a clean cloth, all to be baked in the bread oven. There was of course no electricity and very few people had a decent oven of their own. When the men had deposited their trays, they broke into two groups, one of which would congregate under the horse chestnut tree outside the bakehouse, and the other under the dole tree. At five minutes to eleven, the bakehouse group would disperse, one group to chapel and the other group to church. At 12.30 pm they would go and collect the Sunday lunches that had been cooked for them. The charge for this service was two old pennies.

Today the village is smaller than it used to be. The farms are still there but they don't need as much labour. Some residents are commuters to nearby towns. But village life is alive and well. The village community assembles for its annual rituals; the fete, the sports day, the donkey derby. Modern traffic must sit and wait for the team of morris dancers to finish its display. And the ducks are still swimming on the village pond.

# Twyford

Twyford with a population of approximately 550 is located in north Buckinghamshire just a mile or two from the border with Oxfordshire. It has only one road passing through the village and no major roads or motorways nearby. It is a very quiet and peaceful place in which to live.

It has a very beautiful old church dating back to the 14th

century with some features of an earlier date. The tower, built around 1320, contains a modern clock and a peal of six bells. The doorway and chancel arch are both Norman and in the church-yard an ancient preaching cross can still be seen.

The village also has a few very old houses dating back to the 17th century and one that is 15th century and although many larger, modern houses have been built in recent years the village has not lost its charm. With farms and farmland surrounding it Twyford is never crowded.

Hodges is a name heard many times in the village but as in many villages the aspect of all staying in the village is rapidly changing.

There are many organizations in the village including an active drama group who have entertained the villagers with several pantomimes and perhaps more unusually a group of morris dancers.

# Waddesdon 🦉

Stone Age and Bronze Age tools discovered on or near Lodge Hill, are an indication that people in ancient times occupied the land now known as Waddesdon. Later when the countryside was divided into 'Hundreds' by the Anglo-Saxons, the Hundred of Waddesdon was one of the original portions of Buckinghamshire. The name itself is thought to be derived from the Saxon words Wode (wood) and Don (hill).

The Anglo-Saxon village of Waddesdon stood on the Roman Road, Akeman Street, about five miles from Aylesbury and 11 miles from Bicester.

In 1086 it is recorded in the Domesday Survey that Waddesdon was the largest property held by Miles Crispin, so it is possible that he lived in the village. However, the Lords of the Manor have not normally resided at Waddesdon, and without a big house and newsworthy residents the village earns few mentions in history. The community suffered the effects of the plague and traumas of the Civil War in common with neighbouring villages, but came off worse than most as a result of the Enclosures, when all of the large common fields were lost and very little employment was available. About this time the name 'Black Waddeson' was earned as a result of the hostile reception meted out to travellers.

The turning point in Waddesdon's fortunes arrived when Baron Ferdinand de Rothschild purchased the large manorial estate, and proceeded to construct his country mansion on Lodge Hill in 1874. During the next 25 years many changes were wrought in Waddesdon, the village itself was practically rebuilt, half of it removed a few hundred yards nearer to Aylesbury. Employment prospects improved as dozens of jobs became available in the house, and on the gardens and farms of the estate. Social life in every form of physical recreation and enlightenment was encouraged and assisted. Instead of being the place to avoid, Waddesdon became acceptable at all levels. The Baron entertained politicians, artists and royalty; the Prince of Wales was a regular visitor, even Queen Victoria came to see what the Baron had achieved – and made much of the novelty of electric lights!

Some of the older villagers can recall Waddesdon before the First World War when the village was pre-eminent in the area for every aspect of life. The Parish Church and three Non-Conformist Chapels thrived, two brass bands and a Philharmonic Society were admired by all, and the football and cricket teams reigned supreme. More than 60 part or full-time businesses ensured the self-sufficiency of the community. Services available included several bakers and provisioners, a photographer, a rat-catcher, a gas works, builders and numerous 'front room' shops selling a wide range of small items; cottons, threads, sweets, etc. Few villagers had need to stray farther than the parish boundaries.

This seemingly idyllic and rather unusual village still found an enthusiasm for some of the old traditions including the annual Feast Day in October, and the seven yearly perambulation of the parish boundary. Sadly the Feast Day has faded away, but Beating the Bounds of the combined parishes of Waddesdon, Westcott and Wrodham is very enthusiastically carried out. Taking two days to cover the course, the 'Bounders' still follow the tradition at Rogationtide of marking the boundary and spanking young boys over the marks 'to impress the place upon them'.

After the Second World War several council housing estates were built, but unlike most neighbouring villages Waddesdon has not experienced large private housing developments. The majority of the land still belongs to the manor and the church as it has since the enclosures. The population has remained around 2000 as in 1900, and the broad structure of the village has not altered significantly. However it is the role of the village which has changed, along with the lifestyles of the inhabitants.

Most of us leave the village for our work, our provisions and much of our bought entertainment.

Social life in the village has undergone change, thriving sports clubs and other organisations cater for a wider range of members than those of yesteryear. The brass bands and Philharmonic Society are long gone.

In 1957 Waddesdon Manor, its art treasures and the wooded slopes of Lodge Hill, was bequeathed to the National Trust by James de Rothschild. The property is visited by many thousands each year, some of whom take the opportunity to stop for a while in Waddesdon's fine High Street. There they may savour a little of what makes the village somewhat special for the people of Waddesdon.

# Water Eaton

Water Eaton village has seen many changes over the past 50 years. It stood apart from both Bletchley and Fenny Stratford and was only approached by Water Eaton Road and Manor Road which were mere country lanes with high hedges and trees on either side.

Water Eaton still only boasts one public house – the Plough. The original Plough was a small slated building together with several outbuildings. Alongside was the village pond, now vanished. Opposite was the village green, which still remains, but is no longer encircled by a hedge.

Coronation Hall, adjacent to the green was built on the site of the old village school which stood until the 1920s. The school house still remains joining the hall. Coronation Hall too has seen many changes. It served as a billet for the Army in the Second World War. Today it plays host to many social functions.

There are still old cottages remaining in Mill Road. Four of them are elegantly thatched and preserved, and are listed buildings. The village pump was situated in Mill Road and standing proudly on the corner was the big old hollow oak tree. Oh! what a delight that was for the children. Sadly both the oak tree and the pump have gone.

The canal still continues its course. Once it was a hive of

activity. Barges regularly used the wharf for loading and unloading their cargo. Modern bungalows with gardens stretching to the canal occupy this site. Boats are moored alongside, signs of a more affluent age. Pleasure cruises are now a feature of the canal, as are pleasant walks along the tow path where the fishermen wait patiently for the fish to bite.

Over the canal bridge is Water Eaton Mill. Years ago this was in regular use with water flowing into the mill stream. It served as the local pleasure and leisure area. Children happily paddled and bathed and many took their first swimming lessons there. Alas! It has been allowed to dry up and weeds and undergrowth have taken over.

Since the Second World War housing estates have been erected. The largest is the Lakes Estate covering a wide area of what was once lush green fields with cows quietly grazing. With more housing there has been an increase in population and in volume of traffic. There still remains a part of Water Eaton very much akin to a village, its identity not lost, although it now joins Bletchley and Fenny Stratford and is incorporated within the designated area of the new city of Milton Keynes.

# Weedon

Weedon lies about half a mile to the east of the road from Aylesbury to Buckingham, about three miles north of Aylesbury. Some 350 people live in the village, in 140 houses, the oldest probably being the Manor farmhouse, which carries several dates in the 1640s on its walls. Several families have lived in Weedon for many generations; the Fleets for 200 or so years, the Finchers for upwards of a hundred.

By the main crossroads is the tiny village green, and Five Elms Inn, which is thatched like several of its neighbours. Beside the Five Elms a lane called Stockaway leads to the village pond.

Although the name Weedon means 'A place of heathen worship' the village has the distinction of having been the location of the first place in Buckinghamshire licensed for Methodist services, and John Wesley himself is said to have preached from a mound near the crossroads. Now there is a Methodist church, and a dedicated sanctuary in part of the Old Schoolroom, where Anglican services are regularly held. There are some traces of monastic ruins in the grounds of the Lilies to the north west of the village, but there is no material evidence to support the legend that there was once a convent called the Roses at the south east end, in the grounds of Weedon Lodge.

In the mid-19th century Lord Nugent, younger brother of the Duke of Buckingham lived in the Lilies, and it is rumoured that in his time the local militia used to march from a row of cottages still locally known as the Barracks, to be drilled on the Lilies lawn. Although the house was rebuilt in 1870, the fleur-de-lys has been retained in the porch as a reminder that Louis Philippe was expected to spend his years of exile from France there, but he went to another house near Aylesbury.

In the 19th century the village was almost self-supporting. Most of the men worked on the farms or at the Lilies, and the women and girls worked as domestics or as lace makers and straw plaiters for hats. There was a baker, a butcher, a blacksmith, bricklayers and carpenters, and a tailor, and there were several small shops. Nowadays apart from farmers and farm workers, most people travel to Aylesbury or further afield to work.

Since the Queen's Silver Jubilee there has been increased social activity, and a Village Association has been formed, run by a voluntary committee, to which all residents automatically belong. The Association organises an annual garden party, Christmas parties, a horticultural show and various other events throughout the year.

# Wendover 🌿

Wendover isn't just a pretty place. As with an interesting person, it has character as well as looks. Described as enjoying 'unsurpassed views of the Chiltern Hills', Wendover is situated at the foot of the escarpment on the edge of the Vale of Aylesbury and the High Street lies along a fragment of the ancient Icknield Way. Today, walkers with packs on their backs can be seen, winter and summer, swinging into their stride as they pass through Wendover as they retrace the old road.

Famous names have been associated with Wendover. John Hampden who opposed the imposition of ship money which triggered off the Civil War, and Edmund Burke, represented Wendover as M.P.s in 1623 and 1796 respectively, and John Colet, founder of St Paul's School, London, whose father was twice Lord Mayor of London. The notorious hanging Judge Jeffreys stayed in Wellwick House (the lane to which is said to be the haunt of the Wendover ghost).

In the past the women of Wendover were occupied in splitting and plaiting straw for the Luton hat trade and with the making of Bucks lace. Today this sort of occupation is more likely to be taking place at one of the W.I.s or at evening classes.

Wendover has many interesting buildings including two mills, one of which is an unusual tower-windmill, now sail-less and converted to a dwelling house. A resident of ninety, whose father worked at the windmill pointed out the mill cottage in which he was born – what continuity! There are some lovely houses of various periods. Some are thatched, as are the 16th century Cold-Harbour cottages given to Katherine of Aragon as part of her dowry, by Henry VIII. There are Georgian, Victorian and such new constructions as the attractive Health Centre and the modern row of shops called the Tanyard; of extremely pleasing but completely modern design. The name links the old with the new, reminding the contemporary inhabitants of the occupations of their predecessors, when tanning, rope-making, metal-casting and all the industries of a self-supporting community were carried on. Now employment is found in the small industries in the area or in the varied shops or in the places of refreshment which abound in Wendover.

Of the many hostelries the Red Lion has the longest lineage. First licenced 400 years ago, it has boasted the patronage of Oliver Cromwell, Robert Louis Stevenson and poet Rupert Brooke. From here a two-horse bus used to operate to London. Now commuting inhabitants can travel easily by train, the line having just been reprieved from threatened closure. Many people commute to Aylesbury or other towns and villages and the continual increase in road traffic is making the much desired by-pass more urgent. The village being anxious to find the most acceptable and least destructive route so that its individual character and atmosphere can be preserved.

# Westbury 🦌

Westbury is on the south side of the ridge between Brackley and Buckingham, above the river Great Ouse. There are about 350 people and 110 houses, stone cottages and farm houses, some fine stone barns, and modern houses. The church, built in the 12th and 13th centuries, is surrounded by a pleasant graveyard, shaded by fine yew trees.

Until 1930, all the village, except the church and Reindeer public house, belonged to the Manor. Now the Manor House is a boys preparatory school, and most of the houses are owner-occupied.

The Reindeer public house is a pleasant old building, on the main road, where it attracts lunchtime trade from passing cars, but is a meeting place for villagers in the evening, as is the Working Men's Club close by.

At the lower end of the village is the mill, now used as a craft centre with rooms rented by various small enterprises. Nearby are two factories, one making adhesives, the other plastic coatings. These provide some villagers with employment. Although Westbury is surrounded by farm land, very few people are now farm workers. Most work in the neighbouring towns.

# Westcott 🦌

Westcott was a small village in the middle of farming land until the beginning of the Second World War, when a large area to the west was taken over by the Air Ministry for use as an airfield and bomber training unit. Some of the gallant men who flew from here and died on active service are buried in the little village churchyard. After the war, the R.A.F. left and since then the establishment has been used for the development of rocket propulsion. The residents of the village have become accustomed to the occasional bang or roar as a rocket engine is fired. It has now been taken over by the Royal Ordnance Factory.

In 1935, a fund was set up to provide a village hall, money being raised through donations and fetes, but before enough was raised the war started and the fund fell dormant. Various attempts were

172

made after the war to raise more money, but the fund was still far short of the required amount as building and land prices had both soared. It finally proved impossible to reach the desired figure, so the trustees were allowed in 1978 to spend the money on the clearance of an area of common land near to the church and the school for use as a village green and playing field, with swings and other play apparatus for the children of the village.

Until about 1935, the village was served by the Quainton to Brill tramway and many of the older residents have either worked on it, or had relatives who did. The track of the railway can still be traced and the old ticket office and waiting room still stands alongside the station house. Many railway enthusiasts visit West-cott to see and photograph these reminders of a bygone age.

As most of the residents of the village either work at, or have relatives or friends who work at, the Ministry establishment, many use the social and sporting facilities of the establishment for recreational and entertainment activities.

# Weston Turville 🐝

Weston Turville is a small village nestling under the Chiltern Hills, between Wendover and Aylesbury.

At the turn of the century the main occupation for the menfolk of the village was breeding white Aylesbury ducks for the London markets. There were ponds everywhere; the main one being in Main Street, opposite the village shops, where the bus shelter now stands and a house still remains known as 'Pond Farm'. The women and girls were engaged in the making of straw plait for the Luton hat industry.

The church of St Mary, part of it dating back to the 13th century, has a small fragment of medieval glass including a Madonna and Child, on a brilliant blue background, the rest of the stained glass having been destroyed by Cromwell's soldiers.

Also in the church hangs the 'Will of Widow Turpin' and reads thus:

The Widow Turpin's Gift
She gave all her freehold leasehold arable land and lay ground lying and being within the Parish and Common fields of

Weston in the County of Bucks with all Commons and Profit there into belonging to Mary Hockley, for the term of her natural life and no longer and if she hath any children lawfully begotten on her Body, then they too have her land and lay ground aforesaid equally divided betwixt them and for want of such issue then immediately after her decease. She gave all the aforesaid estate to the 'Poor of Weston' aforesaid for ever; and that the overseerers of the Poor of the said Parish of Weston and their successors shall at the best rate and for the most profit they can, let all the said estate and the rents of the same shall be laid out only two shillings for their trouble, in great loaves of good and wholesome bread to be equally distributed by them to the poorest inhabitants of the aforesaid Parish by equal portions on the feast of St Michael the Arch Angel and the Annunciation of the Blessed Virgin Mary.

The gift became due in the year 1736.

Nowadays there are no real poor in the village, but tokens for bread or flour are given to a number of elderly widows.

An epitaph in the churchyard recalls the local tragedy of two brothers: James and Frederick Bates in 1868. They were drowned when they fell through the ice on Mill Pond. It reads:-

'They sank beneath the frozen wave
None to rescue none to save
Tempted to death in a sportive play
These brothers sleep on Jesus Day.'

The Manor House was built in the early part of the 18th century and enlarged in about 1830. There is evidence of Roman occupation, as during 1855 a Roman emphora was excavated from the adjoining rectory and a fine gold Viking ring was found, now in the British Museum. There in the grounds, the motte and bailey can still be seen. The fortifications were dismantled by order of Henry II, after the 1173–1174 rebellion, but the de Turville family continued to live there until the reign of King John. The village of Weston then became known as Weston Turville. The present owner of the manor is Noel Edmonds, the TV presenter, his helicopter being a familiar sight these days.

There have been many changes over the years but Weston Turville is still a thriving delightful village to live in.

# Weston Underwood 🐦

'We dwell in a neat and comfortable abode, in one of the prettiest villages in the kingdom', wrote William Cowper, the poet, in 1786 having moved to the Lodge at Weston Underwood from Olney.

In the Domesday Book it is recorded as Westone and was then in the hands of the Bishop of Constance, the Earl of Morton and the Countess Judith, niece of the Conqueror, passing on to the Biduns, Peyvres and Bosuns and thence to the Olney family. Weston House belonged to the Throckmortons, a Roman Catholic family who acquired the estate through the marriage of Sir Thomas Throckmorton to Margaret, daughter and heir of Sir Robert Olney of Weston Underwood in 1446. The estate remained in the possession of the Throckmorton family until 1898 when it was bought by Lieut. Col. W. G. Bowyer. Sir Charles Throckmorton had previously acceded to the principal seat of the family at Coughton in Warwickshire and Weston House, dilapidated and decayed was pulled down in 1827. The old stables crowned with clock tower and cupola still remain and have long since been converted into living accommodation.

The wilderness through which Cowper and Mrs Unwin were able to walk, by permission of the Throckmortons is now owned and used by Mr Christopher Marler for breeding and rearing exotic birds and animals threatened in the wild. The grounds still contain the small temple, statues and pedestals with urns inscribed with lines by Cowper.

The large barn opposite the Elm Grove through which Cowper saw 'the thresher at his task' is now converted into two houses. At the entrance to the park and grounds from the village side is a large stone 17th century gateway, with piers surmounted by vases with pines, known locally as the 'Knobs', through which the road now runs to Olney.

Weston Lodge, the 17th century house where William Cowper lived from 1786–1795 looks as elegent as it did in his day. It is stone-built with 13 sash windows and three dormers in the tiled roof. It was on one of the bedroom shutters at the back of the house that he wrote the following words before leaving for East Dereham in 1795:

'Farewell, dear scenes, for ever closed to me,
Oh, for what sorrows must I now exchange ye!

In Cowper's time and all through the 19th century lacemaking was a cottage industry as in all Buckinghamshire villages. The women and children worked very long hours for little money. As the children worked at their pillows in the lace schools they chanted in sing-song voices the lace tells which helped them count the number of pins placed in an hour. Their proficiency was measured in this way. One tell sung at Weston Underwood was:

'A lad down at Weston looked over a wall,
And saw nineteen little golden girls playing at ball.
Golden girls, golden girls, will you be mine,
You shall neither wash dishes nor wait on the swine,
But sit on a cushion and sew a fine seam,
Eat white bread and butter and strawberries and cream.'

The 'golden girls' were the gold-headed pins that marked the footside of the lace. The word nineteen runs in many of the tells being the number at which counting often commenced. Bobbins too were often inscribed with names and sayings.

When the wives and children were lacemaking most of the men would be working in the fields or at the large houses in the village. Others would be working at their trades as a butcher, baker, shoemaker, carpenter, blacksmith, tailor or shopkeeper. Most villages were self-sufficient at this time.

In 1864 the population of Weston Underwood was 398, to-day it is around 190. Families are much smaller and very few people work on the land compared with a hundred years ago. Many of the smaller cottages have been enlarged by knocking two or even three into one. Twenty years ago the village consisted of many elderly people and very few children. To-day a generation later very few of the old village families remain but younger families are now moving in bringing new life to the village.

# West Wycombe 🦚

Mentioned in the Domesday Book, the Manor of Wicumbe (West Wycombe) was held by Wakelin, Bishop of Winchester and was and is for the supplies of the monks of the Church of Winchester. There were 27 villagers, 8 smallholders and 7 slaves! There were also 3 mills on the river Wye which passes through the village, a fishery with a thousand eels and a thousand pigs kept.

The village has remained unspoilt because until the early part of this century it formed part of the West Wycombe Estate which was purchased by the Dashwood family in 1698. Sir Francis Dashwood was created Premier Baronet of Great Britain in 1707 and thus forged the links with the family and village which continue to the present day. The present Baronet, another Sir Francis, is the

eleventh holder of the title. In the middle of the 18th century, the second Baronet undertook the re-building of his country home, following the Italian Palladian style of architecture, bringing painters from Italy to carry out this work. He also re-built and enlarged the ancient parish church on the hill opposite his House in the same style and the church tower was topped with the Golden Ball – a copy of a similar one to be found on the Customs Building at Venice.

In 1929 a large portion of the village was purchased by the Royal Society of Arts which repaired and modernised the houses which date from the 16th and 18th centuries. Later, in 1934, the National Trust acquired these properties from the Royal Society and has continued to maintain the village in its present state.

Older residents remember many incidents of their childhood in the village. Mrs Potter recalls when her family spent many happy times sledging, exploring the caves and climbing on the hill. 'We used to go in the caves and paid one penny for a candle. On one occasion some boys were hiding there and blew our candles out. We were scared, but fortunately we were not too far from the entrance, so soon got out! We often climbed the hill and some brave ones even climbed the church tower. We used to have Sunday School treats on the hill'.

Mrs Fryer remembers choosing a few cheap sweets from Katy Rippington's shop. She was so precise that it is said that she would cut a sweet in half to get the weight exactly right! Mrs Carter's bay window offered further delights. Here, for a halfpenny or even a farthing, Mrs Carter would brush off the flies and wasps from the sweetie boxes and drop a few coveted suckers into a hand-twisted paper cone.

# Whaddon 🌾

This small village stands high on a ridge nearly 500 ft above sea level, overlooking Whaddon Chase with the new city of Milton Keynes in the distance.

The name Whaddon is an old English word for 'Wheat Hill' and the village is mentioned in the Domesday Book.

It is best known as the original home of the Whaddon Chase Foxhounds, started by the Selby-Lowndes family back in the

1800s. Unfortunately this hunt no longer exists, as it has recently been incorporated with the Bicester and Warden Hill Hunt. There is still a lane in the village known as Kennel Lane where the hounds were once kept.

Whaddon Hall was the Manor House for many years and the home of the Lowndes family from 1783 when Mr W. Lowndes Selby took possession of the Hall. In 1813 his son took again the family name of Lowndes after that of Selby, and so the name of Selby-Lowndes became associated with the village and remains in the memory of many of the older villagers.

The present Whaddon Hall is at least the fourth to stand on the site. The Lowndes family left to live in Winslow at the beginning of the Second World War, when the Hall was taken over by the War Office, later to be replaced by the Foreign Office. In the 1960s it became a factory, and, in the 1970s was to be turned into a Country Club, but unfortunately this venture ended with a fire, resulting in the building being gutted, after which it was sold and has now been converted into four luxury apartments with the stable block and the two gate lodges also having been converted into houses.

Across the Parks, due east from the Hall, is the site of Sneshall Priory, a small house for Benedictine Monks dedicated to St Leonard in about 1218. The stone from this priory was used to build the small church of St Giles at Tattenhoe which comes under the benefice of Whaddon and is still used regularly during the summer months.

Whaddon has now got an approximate population of 500. Unlike a few years ago, when most of the village people worked at Wolverton, either at the British Rail Engineering Works or McCorquodale Printing Works, with many working in agriculture, now only a few are still employed in these industries. With Whaddon becoming a dormitory village to Milton Keynes, people now work in Milton Keynes and surrounding districts or commute to London.

Like most villages, Whaddon has changed over the years from being almost self supporting by having its own bakery, butcher's shop, blacksmith and tailor, to the village life we have today.

# Whelpley Hill 🖎

The Romans made a camp on the hill now known as Whelpley Hill, situated high up on the edge of the Chilterns. The Romans moved on and for a while the little place slumbered. Later a little hamlet developed. Through all the changes in the following centuries the little hamlet has survived.

A major change to the village's traditional way of life came with the Second World War. Our menfolk took up arms and uniforms joining the defence volunteers. Evacuees were made welcome and quickly absorbed into village life. Everyone at home was busily involved in first aid classes, fitting gas masks and raising money for the war effort. Then, suddenly, there came the bulldozers carving huge swathes through the standing corn. Unbelievably, we heard that our village was to become part of an airfield. Large areas of concrete were laid criss-crossing the village. What was happening? It looked as if we were to be cut off from the outside world. Barriers were erected at each end of the village but we were told we would be issued with passes to allow us to leave and enter. So the villagers watched and waited.

A few weeks later some American servicemen arrived to prepare the area for operation as a bomber airfield. On a sunny afternoon we watched the arrival of the 'Flying Fortresses' which, after landing, moved to their dispersal points, four of them only fifty yards away from our Village Hall. The local lads soon adopted their favourite plane, for each had a name painted on the side, such as *Yankee Doodle*, *Friday the 13th*, *Memphis Belle*, *Johnny Reb* and *Bad Penny* to name but a few. Friendly relations between the crews and villagers soon developed, especially in our Village Hall. We danced and we sang together. It was our boast that we never had any trouble. Preparations went on apace for bombing operations. Each morning at dawn we were awakened by the roar of engines as the aircraft were readied for take off for that day's target. Some did not return, their parking place empty. The village mourned. Many well known faces appeared around the village, Clark Gable, Glen Miller, Bob Hope, James Stewart and William Holden, to name a few.

In September 1944 the bombers left the airfield, their places taken over by the Air Transport Service, whose task it was to return the American servicemen to the U.S.A. In a few months the war ended. The village gradually settled down to its normal quiet ways. Concrete dispersals and runways fell into disuse. The barriers were down. The land was eventually given back to the farmers.

Only the old runways remain, weeds and scrub growing freely between the cracks where so much action had taken place. Is it all in the past or does something still remain? Newcomers to the village walking their dogs in the area have experienced a feeling of a 'presence'. Their animals bristle and howl and sometimes run away home. Their owners cannot account for it. Is there something? Who knows? For many of those airmen leaving this airfield on their deadly missions, it was to be their last contact in this world. It makes one think!

# Whitchurch 🌿

Ours is a most friendly village where many human needs are supplied by a baker, builder, grocer, post office, hairdresser, several pubs, a doctor and of course a vicar. In the past there were even more tradesmen including a blacksmith, coalman and a shoemaker who worked with both hands and a mouth full of nails! There are many large houses but gone are the days of 'Master and Servant'. To-day most of the inhabitants, apart from the farmers, work elsewhere.

The May Queen is crowned on Market Hill and with four attendants tours the village in a splendid 1909 Motor Car. The Morris Men dance as their predecessors did and Market Hill, once a trading centre, becomes a place of great amusement. The school children plait ribbons around a Maypole in a nearby garden. A cycle race around the Mound revives something of medieval life, for on this site once stood a castle surrounded by a moat. The famous building was destroyed by Cromwell and the stones were used to repair neigbouring churches, improve roads and supply some of the necessary material to help build many of the lovely cottages in the village to-day.

In our present age cars speed through the High Street and the occupants take little notice of the Old Court building, now an hotel. Across the road is the Whittle Hole: a perennially running spring that never freezes in winter. Before tap water came to the village this was the chief water supply and men wearing wooden yokes carried buckets of water. The inhabitants of a nearby house still use Whittle Hole water and brew the best cup of tea in the village.

The village stands high and commands splendid views of the county and beyond, as Rex Whistler's painting *The Vale from Whitchurch* will testify.

The church is the most important building full of interest and many craftsmen's marks can be seen on the pillars. The bells in the tower, as of old, are rung by local people. Nearby stands an old house, once inhabited by monks and centuries later became tenement homes but now it is a cared-for dwelling with a lovely walled garden. Across the road stands a stone-built chapel which houses an organ once owned by the Duke of Wellington. Both church and chapel people meet together and a feeling of unity lingers. Another chapel, no longer needed, houses the fire engines and most of the fire-fighters are local people.

The Hounds always frequented the village and the old people recall King Edward VII attending a Meet at Beechmoor. To-day there are difficulties, some caused by protestors and some by modern ways of life and the pack has united with neighbours. We still see Hounds but not so often.

Whitchurch with its white stone church on the hill adds its share in so many ways to the life and charm of Buckinghamshire.

# Wing 🐝

The name Wing comes from the Anglo Saxon 'Weowungum' meaning Weowum's People, gradually becoming Wenge and finally Wing. Standing on a ridge rising from the Vale of Aylesbury it must be one of the oldest inhabited sites in the county. Its church of All Saints was begun in the 10th century and has massive Saxon arches. It was called by Sir John Betjeman 'The most important Saxon church in the country.' There are numerous monuments and brasses including one to Thomas Cotes, porter at Ascott Hall 1648.

The Manor of Wing has been held by many different noble families through the ages, including the Crown. Some of the names have been used in the new housing estates – Chesterfield, Overstone, Wantage, Dormer etc. A charter was granted in 1255 by Henry III for a weekly Thursday market, and for a 3 day Michaelmas Fair. In the Domesday Book, Wing was worth 5 hides – today it has a population of 2800.

Although pleasant it is not a picture postcard village, and is eagerly awaiting the promised by-pass to cure the traffic problems. Only a few buildings are really old – these include: the Cock and the Queens' Head, the Almshouses, the Old Rectory and a number of cottages. The remainder are mostly 19th century brick terraces with much modern infilling, and housing estates on the outskirts. The Almshouses were founded in 1596 by Dame Dorothy Pelham, widow of Sir William Dormer, Lord of the Manor, and have recently been renovated. Princess Elizabeth is said to have slept at the Manor in 1544 on her way from Woodstock to Hampton Court, and Charles I in 1645 on his way to Oxford. The next day a soldier was hanged for stealing Church Plate – local folklaw insists it was a Roundhead!

Dr Richard Dodd became vicar in 1775, but was largely absent, preferring a lively time in London. Two years later he was hanged at Tyburn for forging a bond for £4,200.

During the 18th and 19th centuries the village was said to be very poor. Lace making and straw plaiting by the women helped family finances, the Cock Inn being the receiving centre, with a special room where plaiting could be done in company.

In 1874 Mr Leopold de Rothschild bought a timbered farmhouse at nearby Ascott, greatly enlarging it in the same style. A variety of substantial cottages were built to house estate workers, and Wing became a typical 'Rothschild village' with nearly all employment and activities revolving around the estate. Many distinguished people came to Ascott House including King George V and Queen Mary, who were regularly driven by carriage to church. Edward, Prince of Wales, hunted from there, the school children being given extra lunch time to cheer him. Mr de Rothschild brought his staghounds to Wing, and until recently the Whaddon Chase Foxhounds were kennelled at Ascott. Mrs de Rothschild took a great interest in the village, setting up a small Cottage Hospital (Charlotte Cottage, now used as a health centre) and presenting school prizes and presents at Christmas – notably boots for children with good school attendance. Ascott House and its beautiful 30 acre gardens are now owned by the National Trust and open to the public.

A large village hall was built in 1905, adminstered by the Estate and has only recently been handed to the village. Many activities take place here.

In 1976 when the last open field in the middle of the village was threatened by builders, the Parish Council bought it as a public open space, naming it Jubilee Green, where the children can play safe from traffic. A yearly Carnival and Fete there ends a week of various fund raising activities in the summer, with a Christmas bonfire and carol singing, all arranged by a local committee.

A very successful broadsheet *Whats on in Wing* is now printed and delivered monthly by volunteers and financed by sponsorship, helping to integrate new comers.

# Wingrave 🌿

Wingrave is a hilltop village 5 miles north east of Aylesbury. It was first mentioned in the 9th century when a chapel was built at Withun's Grove (Withun's Wood). The main part of the original village surrounds the church on top of the hill where there is a pleasant green, a village pond and recreation ground with a splendid view of the Chilterns. The recreation ground was given to the village in 1922 by Lord Dalmeny, afterwards the 6th Lord Rosebery, of nearby Mentmore.

The population is about 1200, including a fair proportion of children. The inhabitants work in Aylesbury or Leighton Buzzard, with a few commuting daily to London, while the main employer in the village itself is the MacIntyre School, an establishment for mentally retarded children.

The parish church of SS. Peter and Paul stands on top of the hill and is easily visible from the surrounding vale. The present building dates from the 13th century and has some medieval wall-paintings hidden in a narrow passage off the chancel. The church has a peal of six bells and there is an ancient 15th century bell standing at the base of the tower, near the font which dates from 1190 and is the oldest item in the church.

The most famous local family connected with Wingrave are the Rothschilds, originally residing at Mentmore Towers and including Wingrave in the estate. In 1876 Hannah Rothschild built about 25 houses for farm workers in Wingrave, each bearing her insignia 'H de R' and the date. These are now all privately owned. In the 1860s she built Wingrave its very first school, later known as the Church Rooms and now divided into private dwellings. Mentmore Towers later passed into the hands of the Rosebery family and is now the British HQ of the Transcendental Meditation Movement.

In Victorian times the Stewart-Freeman family were well-known in the county and lived in the manor house of Wingrave. In 1905 there was a great scandal locally when the eldest Stewart-Freeman daughter eloped with the 8th Earl of Essex. The son born to them, Reginald, eventually became the 9th Earl of Essex, and lived with his wife at Floyds Farm, Wingrave, for some years. During the Second World War the manor house was occupied by the exiled Czech Government under Dr Eduard Benes. In gratitude for the hospitality they had received, the Czech Government built the bus shelter at the crossroads for the benefit of travellers. The manor house is today the MacIntyre School.

In the 1880s a Wingrave musician, George Griffin, composed an oratorio called *Samuel* and many hymn tunes. He was also the local postmaster and village baker. Earlier, in 1786, a wealthy Wingrave lady became famous when, lost in a storm between Wingrave and Rowsham, she was directed safely home by the ringing of the church bells. In thankfulness she directed that hay from her two fields should be spread on the church floor for the benefit of the congregation every year at the Patronal Festival on 29th June. This custom has been faithfully maintained every year since then, 1986 being the 200th anniversary.

Wingrave seems a healthy place in which to live, apparently conferring long life on its inhabitants. The oldest man in the village is well over ninety and there are numerous octogenarians. It is a busy and friendly community interested not only in its own occupations and life but also in general charitable enterprises including raising money for cancer research, Save the Children and for the establishment of a hospice in Aylesbury.

# Winslow 🐾

The Mercian King Offa had a palace and chapel in Winslow, and he conceived the idea of founding a monastery and endowing it to the Manor of Winslow. The Domesday Survey of 1086 notes Wineslai as part of the possession of St Albans Abbey, with the Abbot as Lord of the Manor. In 1235 King Henry III authorised a weekly market, and a fair on the feast day of St Lawrence on the 10th August, for which he granted a charter.

The church, c.1320, has been restored and enlarged by successive generations. Of interest are a collection of bibles, one of which is the 1611 authorised version, and Fox's Book of Martyrs, plus a selection of ancient parish registers. The faded wall murals are said to depict the patron saint of the diocese St Frideswide, and also of note, over the aisle, is a fine 20 candle chandelier dated 1670, and made in Buckingham. St Lawrence has a fine peal of bells. The Sanctus bell dates from 1611, and there is a three hourly carillon of Old St Davids.

Keach's Meeting House was built in 1625, and is the second oldest religious building in Winslow. Keach's was the headquarters of dissenting Baptists. Benjamin Keach introduced congregational singing in this chapel to the fury of the London Baptist Association who condemned it as a 'carnal formality'. For many years the meeting house was secreted away behind other buildings, but the atmosphere of Keach's remains very much as it was in the Puritan era.

Today Winslow is still growing steadily, with the addition of several hundred new houses, but manages to retain its links with the past, with its attractive old thatched houses, its market square and cattle markets and delightful surrounding countryside.

# Wooburn

Little seems to be known of Wooburn prior to the Norman Conquest. The parish was at one time in two parts: Bishop's Wooburn and the Manor of Deyncourt. The Manor of Bishop's Wooburn was given as part of the endowment to the Bishopric of Lincoln between 1066 and 1100 and the Manor of Deyncourt was given to a relative of King William – Walter Deyncourt.

There is today very little evidence of the Manors. Wooburn House, which was on the site of the Bishop's Palace, was used as offices by the War Graves Commission during the Second World War. Eventually it was sold, demolished and replaced by a housing estate. In the 1920s a new road was cut through the old Deyncourt Manor lands, separating the parish church from the fields and the old buildings. There now only remains one old cottage in that area.

Traditionally the parish of Wooburn was separated into several smaller parts with their own identity: The Green, The Town, The Moor, The Common, Cores End and the Bourne End of Wooburn. Berghers Hill at Wooburn Common is a very ancient part of the parish; at one time known as Beggers Hill.

The parish church of Wooburn, dedicated to St Paul, dates from soon after the Norman Conquest but it is generally thought that a church stood on the site much earlier than 1066. Over the years the church has been considerably altered and in 1857 the interior was completely restored.

A very well-known person in the village in the first half of the 1900s was Dr Selborne Bailey who died in 1969. He was a churchwarden from 1928–1969, and very much involved with the church and other local activities. He was in charge of the local fire brigade and at the time local brigades were taken over by civic authorities a film was made of the Wooburn fire fighters for posterity.

When Dr Bailey came to Wooburn he 'inherited' Mr Dash who had driven his predecessor on his rounds in a horse and trap. He became almost as well-known as his employer and soon was at the wheel of a car driving Dr Bailey around the village.

To celebrate Dr Bailey's 50 years as a doctor in the parish in 1961 a window was erected in the parish church, paid for by subscriptions from his patients and friends. He had a very strong sense of humour and at that time he is reputed to have said 'It is not in my memory because I am not dead yet'.

Another well known local figure was Herbert Healey who died in 1953. He was a churchwarden and served for thirty-one years. Herbert Healey was Mayor of High Wycombe 1929/31, a governor of High Wycombe Hospital and a manager for several local schools. He had a furniture factory in High Wycombe and was very prominent in Furniture Trade circles.

The Valley of the Wye was at one time noted for the paper mills though most of these are no longer in existence, Wiggins Teape at Glory Mill being an exception. Instead of Thomas & Green, paper makers at Soho Mill there is today a fairly large industrial estate.

A painting of the village green by Harold W. Boutcher done in 1888, and now hanging in St Paul's parish church, shows that the green is not greatly changed except of course today the shops and houses surrounding it have been modernised and roads built to cater for the present day traffic.

# Worminghall

Worminghall is situated on the border of Buckinghamshire, its near neighbours being Oakley, Ickford and Waterperry.

The oldest building is the church, dedicated to St Peter and Paul. It stands in a field and is approached across a cattle grid which makes it both unusual and in wintertime, somewhat inconvenient. Architecturally, the church is a mixture of 12th, 13th and 14th century styles. It was repaired and restored substantially in the 19th century, mainly financed by the family of Lord Clifden, who held the Manor at that time.

It is in memory of Henry King, Bishop of Chichester, that the Almshouses at the junction of The Avenue with Clifden Road were built by his son John King in 1675. Originally they housed six poor single men and four women, who received 3s 3d a week, a ton of coal at Christmas and the Bread Charity every Sunday with extra bread on Good Friday and at Easter. The men received coats, and the women dresses in alternate years. In the middle of this century, the interiors were modernised and they now comprise six dwellings. The charities are no longer maintained.

The Clifden Arms on the south west edge of the village, is an exceptionally picturesque black and white 16th century pub. The Clifden is becoming increasingly popular as a village meeting place. It hosts the fete which is held on a date as near as possible to the feast of St Peter and Paul, which was originally Worminghall's Feast Day. The market day has long since been completely lost.

In the Second World War, Worminghall was invaded by the Royal Air Force based on the airfield adjacent to the village, flying Wellington bombers. After the war, the empty buildings were taken over by people needing homes and some of the descendants of these people were rehoused in the village and are now, of course, totally absorbed into the village. They still talk about the school bus 'going up the camp' as it used to pick up the children living in the old airfield buildings. The airfield reverted to being a farm, and its runways stored hundreds of British Leyland cars awaiting dispatch all over the world in the 1960s. In 1982, the field sprouted palm trees overnight and convoys of film personnel travelled daily from Oxford to film the James Bond film *Octopussy* and local people played the game of 'Spot Roger Moore', the star of the film.

# Index

Akeley   9
Ashendon   10
Ashley Green   11
Askett (see Monks Risborough)   121
Aston Clinton   12
Astrope (see Long Marston &
   Puttenham)   106

Ballinger   13
Beachampton   14
Bellingdon   15
Bledlow   17
Bledlow Ridge   18
Booker   20
Boarstall (see Oakley)   129
Botolph Claydon (see East & Botolph
   Claydon)   46
Bovingdon Green   20
Bow Brickhill   21
Brill   23
Buckland Common (see Cholesbury
   cum St Leonards)   34
Burnham   24

Cadmore End   25
Cadsden (see Monks Risborough)
   121
Castlethorpe   25
Chackmore (see Dadford)   40
Chalfont St Giles   26
Chalfont St Peter   28
Chearsley   29
Cheddington   30
Chenies   31
Chesham Bois   33
Cholesbury cum St Leonards   34
Coleshill   35
Cublington   37
Cuddington   39

Dadford   40
Denham   41
Dorney   43
Downley   44

Drayton Beauchamp (see Aston
   Clinton)   13
Drayton Parslow   46

East Claydon   46
Edlesborough   49
Ellesborough   51
Emberton   53

Farnham Common   54
Farnham Royal   54
Fingest   56
Flackwell Heath   56
Forty Green   57
Foxcote (see Maids Moreton)   112
Frieth   58
Fulmer   59

Granborough   60
Great Brickhill   60
Great Hampden   62
Great Horwood   63
Great Kimble (see The Kimbles)   88
Great Kingshill   63
Great Linford   65
Great Missenden   65
Grendon Underwood   67
Gubblecote (see Long Marston &
   Puttenham)   106

Haddenham   68
Hambleden   70
Hanslope   71
Hawridge (see Cholesbury cum
   St Leonards)   34
Hazlemere   73
Hedgerley   74
Hitcham   76
Holly Green (see Bledlow)   17
Holmer Green   77
Horn Hill   79
Hughenden   80
Hyde Heath   81

Ibstone   82
Ickford   83
Ilmer (see Longwick)   108
Iver Heath   84
Ivinghoe   86

Jordans   87

The Kimbles   88
Knotty Green   90

Lacey Green   108
Lane End   90
Latimer   90
Leckhampstead   92
Ley Hill   93
Lillingstone Lovell   93
Little Brickhill   96
Little Chalfont   97
Little Hampden   97
Little Horwood   98
Little Kimble (see The Kimbles)   88
Little Kingshill   100
Little Marlow   101
Little Missenden   103
Long Crendon   105
Long Marston   106
Longwick   107
Loosley Row   108
Loughton   110
Lower Cadsden (see Monks
   Risborough)   121
Lower Pollicott (see Ashendon)   10

Maids Moreton   112
Marlow Botton   114
Marsh Gibbon   115
Marsworth   116
Meadle (see Monks Risborough)
   121
Medmenham   116
Mentmore   118
Middle Claydon   119
Monks Risborough   120

Naphill   122
Nash   123
Nether Wichendon   123

Newton Longville   125
Northall (see Edlesborough)   49
North Crawley   126
North Marston   127

Oakley   129
Olney   130
Owlswick (see Longwick)   108

Padbury   131
Penn   133
Penn Street   133
Pitch Green (see Bledlow)   17
Pitstone   135
Prestwood   136
Princes Risborough   137
Puttenham   106

Quainton   139

Radnage   141

St Leonards (see Cholesbury cum
   St Leonards)   34
Seer Green   141
Shabbington   143
Skirmett   144
Skittle Green (see Bledlow)   17
Slapton   144
Soulbury   146
South Heath   13
Speen   147
Steeple Claydon   149
Stewkley   151
Stoke Hammond   153
Stoke Mandeville   154
Stokenchurch   156
Stoke Poges   158
Stowe (see Dadford)   40

Taplow   160
Tattenhoe (see Whaddon)   179
The Lee   162
Thornborough   163
Twyford   165
Tylers Green   133

Upper Pollicott (see Ashendon)   10

191

Verney Junction (see Middle
    Claydon)   119

Waddesdon   166
Water Eaton   168
Weedon   169
Wendover   170
Westbury   172
Westcott   172
Weston Turville   173
Weston Underwood   175
West Wycombe   177
Whaddon   178

Whelpley Hill   180
Whitchurch   181
Whitecliff (see Monks Risborough)
    121
Whiteleaf (see Monks Risborough)
    121
Wing   183
Wingrave   184
Winslow   186
Wooburn   187
Worminghall   188
Wrodham (see Waddesdon)   167

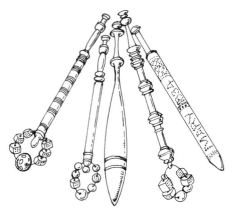

*pillow lace bobbins*